ON THE COVER
Eight- to nine-week old bald eagle nestling. Photograph by Bill Route.

Spatial Patterns of Persistent Contaminants in Bald Eagle Nestlings at Three National Parks in the Upper Midwest

2006-2009

Natural Resource Technical Report NPS/GLKN/NRTR—2011/431

Bill Route

National Park Service
Great Lakes Inventory and Monitoring Network
Ashland, Wisconsin 54806

Paul Rasmussen

Wisconsin Department of Natural Resources
Monona, Wisconsin 53716

Rebecca Key

National Park Service
Great Lakes Inventory and Monitoring Network
Ashland, Wisconsin 54806

Michael Meyer

Wisconsin Department of Natural Resources
Rhinelander, Wisconsin 54501

Mark Martell

Audubon Minnesota
St. Paul, Minnesota 55125

February 2011

U.S. Department of the Interior
National Park Service
Natural Resource Program Center
Fort Collins, Colorado

The National Park Service, Natural Resource Program Center publishes a range of reports that address natural resource topics of interest and applicability to a broad audience in the National Park Service and others in natural resource management, including scientists, conservation and environmental constituencies, and the public.

The Natural Resource Technical Report Series is used to disseminate results of scientific studies in the physical, biological, and social sciences for both the advancement of science and the achievement of the National Park Service mission. The series provides contributors with a forum for displaying comprehensive data that are often deleted from journals because of page limitations.

All manuscripts in the series receive the appropriate level of peer review to ensure that the information is scientifically credible, technically accurate, appropriately written for the intended audience, and designed and published in a professional manner.

Data in this report were collected, analyzed, and interpreted using established, peer-reviewed protocols. This report received formal peer review by subject-matter experts who were not directly involved in the collection, analysis, or reporting of the data, and whose background and expertise put them on par technically and scientifically with the authors of the information.

Views, statements, findings, conclusions, recommendations, and data in this report do not necessarily reflect views and policies of the National Park Service, U.S. Department of the Interior. Mention of trade names or commercial products does not constitute endorsement or recommendation for use by the U.S. Government.

This report is available from the Great Lakes Inventory and Monitoring Network website at (*http://science.nature.nps.gov/im/units/GLKN/monitorreportpubs.cfm*) and the Natural Resource Publications Management website *(http://www.nature.nps.gov/publications/NRPM)*.

Please cite this publication as:

NPS 920/106819, February 2011

Contents

List of Figures

List of Tables

List of Appendices

Executive Summary

During 2006 through 2009 the National Park Service Great Lakes Inventory and Monitoring Network and its partners assessed levels of targeted environmental contaminants in bald eagle (*Haliaeetus leucocephalus*) nestlings at sites in and adjacent to the Apostle Islands National Lakeshore, Mississippi National River and Recreation Area, and St. Croix National Scenic Riverway. Adjacent study areas were added when funds were available for comparisons and these included the entire Wisconsin south shore of Lake Superior and a section of the Mississippi River below Minneapolis-St. Paul, Minnesota, to the southern end of Lake Pepin. A total of 288 bald eagle nestlings were handled, and 154 plasma and 142 breast-feather samples were analyzed for six contaminants: total mercury, lead, DDT (and metabolites DDE and DDD), total PCBs (75 congeners), total PBDEs (9 congeners), and total PFCs (16 analytes). We also archived 123 plasma and 121 feather samples for possible future analysis.

All study areas averaged ≥ 1.0 young per occupied bald eagle nest, considered the threshold for a healthy bald eagle population. The Apostle Islands had the lowest productivity (1.0 in 2008) and the Mississippi National River and Recreation Area had the highest (2.2 in 2006 and 2009). The percent of territories that were successful ranged from 63% at Apostle Islands in 2008 to 100% at the lower St. Croix River (2007 and 2009) and the Mississippi National River and Recreation Area in 2008. Lower productivity on Lake Superior was likely due to lower prey availability compared to other study areas, though some nestlings were subjected to levels of DDE that were above published thresholds and may have suffered sublethal effects.

Contaminant levels varied between study areas and years. The geometric mean ($\bar{x}_{geo}$) mercury levels in feathers ranged from 2.69 ug/g in nestlings on Pools 3&4 of the Mississippi River in 2008 to 7.96 ug/g on the upper St. Croix Riverway in 2006. Mean ($\bar{x}_{geo}$) lead levels in feathers were lowest on the Apostle Islands in 2006 (0.0700 ug/g) and highest in the lower St. Croix River in 2006 (1.03 ug/g). Generally, lead was highest in the lower St. Croix River and along the Mississippi River and lowest on the Apostle Islands and the upper St. Croix Riverway.

Trace levels of DDT in blood were found in seven nestlings from Lake Superior in 2006 and 2007 and in two nestlings from the Mississippi National River and Recreation Area - one in 2006 and one in 2009; DDE was found in all nestlings sampled and at high levels in nestlings from the Apostle Islands in 2006 ($\bar{x}_{geo}$ = 29.7 ug/L). Nestlings on islands furthest from the mainland had among the highest DDE levels all four years. Levels of DDE were lowest on the upper St. Croix River in 2006 ($\bar{x}_{geo}$ = 2.70 ug/L).

Levels of PCBs were lowest on the upper St. Croix River in 2006 ($\bar{x}_{geo}$ = 10.0 ug/L) and highest on the lower St. Croix in 2006 ($\bar{x}_{geo}$ = 139 ug/L).

Polybrominated diphenyl ethers (PBDEs), a group of chemicals of increasing concern, ranged from $\bar{x}_{geo}$ of 1.39 ug/L in the upper St. Croix River in 2006 to $\bar{x}_{geo}$ of 16.8 ug/L in the Mississippi National River and Recreation Area in 2007. Generally, spatial patterns of PBDEs were similar to those of PCBs across the study areas.

Perfluorinated compounds (PFCs), another group of chemicals of increasing concern, were found in all samples, and the primary analyte was PFOS (68% in Mississippi River sample sites and 53% in Lake Superior sample sites by volume). We found PFOS at very high levels in nestlings on the lower St Croix River ($\bar{x}_{geo}$ = 1580 ug/L) and in the Mississippi National River and Recreation Area ($\bar{x}_{geo}$ = 1250 ug/L) in 2006. PFOS was generally low in eaglets from the upper St. Croix Riverway ($\bar{x}_{geo}$ = 13.4 ug/L in 2007) and at moderate levels on the Apostle Islands (146-174 ug/L). A second PFC analyte, PFDS, made up 26% of the PFC volume in eaglet plasma from the Mississippi River study areas but <1% of volume in Lake Superior eaglets. PFOA, another PFC analyte of high interest due to its toxicity and pervasiveness around the world, was found at very low levels in plasma from nestlings in our study areas (<1% of the 16 PFCs by volume); yet it was consistently at its highest levels in nestlings from the Apostle Islands (4.97 ug/L in 2008).

Differences in contaminant burdens between study areas provide insights into the sources, mechanisms of transport, and magnification through the food web. Generally, contaminants associated with industry and municipal waste (PCBs, PBDEs, and PFCs) were highest in bald eagle nestlings near large population centers. However, Lake Superior receives a wide array of pollutants from global sources through air deposition and retains them for longer periods of time; hence, nestlings in remote islands had high levels of some industrial contaminants. The patterns of distribution were further complicated by apparent magnification in the food web at individual nest territories. We theorize that several hot spots of contamination were the result of eagles feeding on prey that were positioned high on the aquatic food web.

Acknowledgments

Major funding for this work was provided by the National Park Service, Great Lakes Inventory and Monitoring Network. In 2008 and 2009 substantial funding was provided by the Minnesota Pollution Control Agency and additional funds were granted by the Donald Weesner Foundation. The Wisconsin Department of Natural Resources conducted occupancy surveys in Wisconsin and the Ramsey County Parks Department contributed staff time for occupancy surveys in Minnesota. Nest tree climbing expertise was provided by the Institute for Wildlife Studies and by Eco-Ascension Research and Consulting. All laboratory analyses on bald eagle samples were conducted by the Wisconsin State Laboratory of Hygiene. The 3M Corporation verified that supplies and equipment were free of PFCs. Numerous employees of the National Park Service and Audubon Minnesota were instrumental in collecting field data and providing logistics. We thank J. Elias, T. Gostomski, S. Hennes, B. Mader, G. Miller, K. Rolfhus, S. Streets, D. VanderMeulen, and J. Wiener for constructive comments on earlier drafts of this report.

Introduction

In the upper Midwestern states of Minnesota, Wisconsin, and Michigan more than 120 million pounds of toxic waste were released into the air, discharged into the water, or disposed on land in 2006 (USEPA 2008). Similar amounts are released annually, and much of this toxic waste ends up in aquatic systems through direct discharge, air deposition, or through ground water inflow. Many of these chemicals, and the metabolites that result from their decomposition, are highly persistent and remain available for up-take by aquatic organisms. Many chemicals that are persistent tend to bioaccumulate and some bio-magnify as they are transferred to organisms higher in the food web. Some of these persistent and bioaccumulative chemicals are also highly toxic to fish, wildlife, and humans (Hudson et al. 1984, Hoffman et al. 2003, Beyer 2011).

The National Park Service (NPS) has a responsibility to understand the levels and potential effects of contaminants from human sources on the natural resources they manage and to inform the visiting public about the potential human health hazards. The NPS Great Lakes Inventory and Monitoring Network (GLKN or Network) began monitoring levels of selected contaminants in 2006. The monitoring involves sampling nestling bald eagles (*Haliaeetus leucocephalus*) to track the bioavailability of targeted contaminants. Bald eagles are high on the aquatic food web and accumulate persistent chemicals, thus acting as effective indicators of contamination.

From the hundreds of chemical contaminants known to occur in the environment, we narrowed our scope to those that are persistent, bioaccumulative, and toxic to fish, wildlife, and humans. We further reduced this list by considering only those chemicals that are of management concern to the NPS units being monitored. Specifically, we selected chemicals that are either (1) the cause of waters within a park being listed in section 303(d) of the Water Quality Act (including fish consumption advisories); (2) listed as a Level I Substance under the Great Lakes Binational Toxics Strategy; or (3) recently identified by state or federal authorities as a new and emerging chemical of concern. We then excluded chemicals that are being adequately monitored by other agencies or that are prohibitively expensive to monitor. The resulting target list is as follows.

- Dichlorodiphenyl-trichloroethane (DDT) and metabolites
  - Dichlorodiphenyl-dichloroethylene (DDE)
  - Dichlorodiphenyl-dichloroethane (DDD)
- Polychlorinated biphenyls (PCBs; including 75 congeners*)
- Total mercury (THg)
- Lead (Pb)
- Perfluorinated compounds (PFCs; including 16 different analytes*)
- Polybrominated diphenyl ethers (PBDEs; including 9 congeners*)

*Congeners and analytes: Some chemicals have several derivatives or molecular variants. For example, PCBs and PBDEs occur as 209 different congeners. Each differs by the number of chlorine or bromine atoms located at specific sites on the molecule. PFC chemistry is more complex and terms vary depending on how the chemical is produced. We use the more general term "analyte" to describe different PFCs. A list of all congeners and analytes measured in this study is provided in Appendix A.

These chemicals have been shown to impact wildlife and humans or have been linked to adverse effects on laboratory animals including reproductive impairment, developmental deformities, neurological disorders, and effects on the endocrine system (Friend and Trainer 1970, Hudson et al. 1984, Nisbet 1989, Noble and Elliot 1990, Bowerman et al. 1994, Gilbertson et al. 1998, Hoffman et al. 2003, Beyer and Meador 2011).

Reproductive failure and population declines of many species of predatory birds were documented in the decades following the introduction of the organochlorine pesticide DDT in North America in 1946 (Gerrard and Bortolotti 1988). When DDT breaks down the metabolites DDE and DDD are formed. DDE is linked to egg-shell thinning, which caused eggs to break when adult birds attempted to incubate them (Nisbet 1989). With the ban of DDT in 1972 many bird populations began to recover (Newton 1979). Yet, through at least the early 1980s the productivity of bald eagles in the Great Lakes region was inversely correlated with levels of DDE and PCBs found in their eggs (Wiemeyer et al. 1984) and in blood plasma of nestlings (Bowerman et al. 2003). These chemicals may no longer limit bald eagle populations in Lake Superior (Dykstra et al. 2005, Dykstra et al. 2010) or the Upper Mississippi River valley (Wiener and Sandheinrich 2010), yet recovery has not been uniform. For example, bald eagles nesting along the shoreline of the Great Lakes have had lower reproductive success than inland populations in Minnesota, Wisconsin, and Michigan (Kozie and Anderson 1991, Dykstra et al. 1998, Bowerman et al. 2003, Wiener and Sandheinrich 2010).

A portion of the contaminants in the upper Midwest are from past use and emissions. Indeed DDT can take more than 30 years to degrade in the cold, clay soils found in some areas of the upper Midwest (ATSDR 2002). However, long-range transport can account for a significant fraction (Engstrom and Swain 1997). Although DDT was banned for sale in North America, it continues to be used in other parts of the world and is found in remote regions of the globe (Nash et al. 2008). Long range atmospheric transport, ingestion and subsequent infusion in the food web by transcontinental-migrant birds, and occasional illegal releases, continue to inoculate aquatic systems with this highly toxic chemical (Stickel et al. 1984, Kannon et al. 2006).

PCBs have a similar story: following high use and disposal in the 1950s and 1960s they were banned in 1979 (Rapaport and Eisenreich 1988). By the 1980s concentrations of PCBs had dropped significantly, though they continued to fluctuate in biota of the Great Lakes basin (Knobeloch et al. 2008). Yet the mixture of PCB congeners found in the environment today differs from the commercial products used in the past (Bush et al. 1984, Hooper et al. 1990). Through time the natural decomposition of PCB congeners continuously changes the mixture that is present in the environment, conserving the more highly chlorinated, enzyme-inducing congeners, and increasing potential toxicity five to 10-fold as they move up the food chain (Hornbuckle et al. 2005).

Mercury (Hg) and lead (Pb) are heavy metals with long histories of human use resulting in widespread contamination. Mercury has been released into the environment for more than a century as a byproduct of cinnabar mining (historically used as a red pigment) and during the mercury-amalgamation process used to extract gold and silver from ore (Wiener et al. 2003). More recently, the Minnesota Pollution Control Agency (MPCA 2004) estimated that in 2000, 50% of the mercury emissions in Minnesota were from energy production (mostly coal burning power plants); 29% was from incineration and disposal of commercial products; and 21% was from taconite processing, pulp and paper processing, and soil roasting. Mercury emissions from Minnesota-based sources declined 68% from 1995 to 2000 (MPCA 2004). Yet mercury emissions from international sources may increase with coal-fired power plants coming on-line in China, India, and other countries (U. S. Energy Information Administration 2010).

Methylmercury (MeHg) is formed when inorganic mercury is deposited on land and water and then methylated by anaerobic bacteria in wetlands and sediments. Methylmercury biomagnifies in aquatic food webs and is highly toxic (Wiener et al. 2003). Laws regulating mercury emissions have led to reductions, yet it remains one of the most pervasive environmental contaminants in the upper Midwest and across the North American continent. All states in the region have issued advisories for fish-consumption in some or all waters (USEPA 2005).

Lead is a neurotoxin that was used as an additive for gasoline and paints beginning in the 1920s. The U. S. Environmental Protection Agency (USEPA) began regulating use of lead in 1973 leading to a total ban on its use in gasoline for on-road vehicles in 1996 under the Clean Air Act. Yet lead poisoning continues to be a concern in wildlife. The National Wildlife Health Laboratory in Madison, Wisconsin, analyzed records of 1,429 bald eagle mortalities across the United States during 1963 – 1984 and found lead poisoning to be the third greatest cause of mortality (11%), exceed only by gunshot and other traumatic injuries. Lead poisoning in bald eagles was believed almost entirely from ingestion of lead pellets when preying or scavenging on crippled or unretrieved waterfowl (Pattee and Hennes 1983). In a retrospective analysis of 138 lead poisoned eagles spanning the years before and after federal regulations on the use of lead shot for waterfowl hunting, Kramer and Redig (1997) found that the prevalence of lead poisoning did not change although the mean levels of lead in poisoned eagles did. In a follow up analysis, Redig et al. (2009) added 12 years of data to the previous 16 years and found a temporal-spatial association with eagle poisonings and the onset of deer hunting season, lead isotope ratios in poisoned eagles were similar to ammunition, and levels of copper in kidneys of poisoned eagles that implied ingestion of copper-jacketed rifle bullets. Although lead shot was banned for waterfowl hunting in 1991, it is still widely used in ammunition for hunting terrestrial species and lead is still widely used in fishing tackle. Its continued use has prompted recent concern for wildlife poisonings including the endangered California condor (Pain et al. 2008).

Perfluorinated compounds (PFCs) and polybrominated diphenyl ethers (PBDEs) are large chemical groups that are of increasing concern in the upper Midwestern United States and around the world (Renner 2000). PFCs have been widely used in a variety of industrial and commercial products such as water, oil, and grease repellents for fabrics (e.g., Scotchgard™), fire-fighting foams, cookware (e.g., Teflon™), polyurethane production, and surfactants. Two PFCs are of particular concern: perfluorooctane sulfonate (PFOS) and perfluorooctanoic acid (PFOA), because they are highly persistent in the environment and bioaccumulate in biota (Giesy and Kannan 2001). The toxicity of PFC compounds is still being defined but PFOS and PFOA have been linked to alterations in thyroid hormone production, liver damage, immune-suppression, and carcinogenesis (summarized by Minnesota Department of Health [MDH] 2010). Because of the global distribution of some perfluorinated compounds, the 3M Company based in St. Paul, Minnesota, phased out production of 8-carbon PFCs, including PFOS and PFOA, in 2000 and ceased production entirely in 2002. However, they continue to produce the shorter-chain C4 and C6 compounds and these and other PFCs can degrade in the environment with PFOS as one of the primary degradation products (Newman and Unger 2003).

PBDEs are similar in structure to PCBs and are widely used as flame retardants in plastic components of computers and televisions, in circuit boards, vehicle upholstery, and many textiles. These chemicals are released during production, product use, and disposal (Kim et al. 2006). PBDEs are now ubiquitous in the environment and are found in human breast milk, marine mammals, birds, fish, sediments, and house dust (Ikonomou et al. 2002, Stapleton et al. 2005, Ismail et al. 2009, Chen and Hale 2010, Fernie and Letcher 2010). The toxicity of PBDEs to humans is unknown, but based on animal studies, the USEPA lists decaBDE as a possible carcinogen. According to the Agency for Toxic Substances and Disease Registry (ATSDR), laboratory animals fed moderate amounts of lower brominated PBDEs have shown effects on the thyroid and liver and animals fed PBDEs as infants have shown subtle behavioral changes. It is not known whether similar effects occur in humans.

The above persistent, bioaccumulative, toxicants (PBTs) are the focus of this monitoring program. Specifically, the monitoring program is designed to answer the following questions:

1) What is the direction and magnitude of change in concentrations of DDT (including metabolites DDE and DDD), total PCBs, total PFCs, and total PBDEs in blood plasma, and of total mercury and lead in feathers, from nestling bald eagles within the monitored study areas?
2) What is the incidence of addled eggs, dead nestlings, and developmental deformities in nestling bald eagles within the study areas?
3) What is the direction and magnitude of change in the number of young produced per occupied bald eagle nest within the study areas?
4) Are the production of bald eagles and the incidences of addled eggs, dead nestlings, and developmental deformities correlated with exposure to the monitored contaminants in the study areas?

Methods

Study Areas

Apostle Islands National Lakeshore

The Apostle Islands National Lakeshore (APIS or Lakeshore) is located on Lake Superior in extreme northern Wisconsin (Figure 1). This island archipelago is administered by the National Park Service to preserve a 19 km (12 mi) mainland segment of the Lake Superior shoreline and 21 islands with a combined Lake Superior shoreline of 257 km (160 mi) and combined land area of 28,086 ha (69,372 acres). The islands extend 24 km (16 mi) from the mainland into the lake and range in size from 1.2 ha (three acres) to 4,000 ha (10,000 acres). The Lakeshore is at the northwestern limits of the northern hardwood forest and contains elements of the southern boreal forest. There are about 20 km (12 mi) of perennial streams and 11 lagoons covering 43 ha (106 acres) in the Lakeshore.

The area surrounding APIS has a low human population density. According to the 2005 U.S. census there were 26 people / mi^2 (10 / km^2) in the 710 mi^2 (1,839 km^2) area that includes four zip codes immediately adjacent to APIS. The NPS estimates that approximately 190,000 persons visit APIS each year.

There is very little heavy industry in the area though a coal-burning power plant is located in Ashland, 17.6 km (10.9 mi) from the APIS boundary. Moraska-Lafrancois and Glase (2005) reported only three industrial dischargers within three miles (4.8 km) of APIS. In addition to direct discharge, however, the total surface area of Lake Superior (82,100 km^2) and its large drainage basin (127,700 km^2) acts as a large receptor of chemicals that are aerially transported from regional and global sources.

Lake Superior's South Shore

The Lake Superior south shore (LSSS) study area is a 238 km long, 8 km wide strip of the Lake Superior shoreline in extreme northern Wisconsin extending from the Superior/Duluth Harbor to the Michigan border (an additional 21 km of Wisconsin shoreline within the APIS study area is not included in this estimate; Figure 1). Use of an 8 km strip along the shoreline is consistent with past studies on contaminants in eagles (e.g., Dykstra et al. 1995) and is generally believed to hold eagle territories that are primarily associated with feeding on Lake Superior. The vegetation is mixed conifer and hardwood.

The twin port cities of Duluth, Minnesota, and Superior, Wisconsin, have a combined population of just over 110,000 (2006 estimate; U.S. Census Bureau). Ashland, Wisconsin, is the next largest community with 8,600 people and five smaller communities each have <1000 people. Ownership is a mixture of state, county, Tribal (Red Cliff and Bad River Bands of Chippewa), and private.

Major point sources for contaminants are industry in Superior and Duluth and a large municipal landfill near shore about 1 km east of Superior. Ashland has a coal-fired power plant and a Superfund site where soil, ground water, and Lakefront sediments are contaminated with polynuclear aromatic hydrocarbons and volatile organic compounds. Additionally, as with the

APIS study area, the size of Lake Superior and its basin area receive chemicals that are aerially transported from the region and globally.

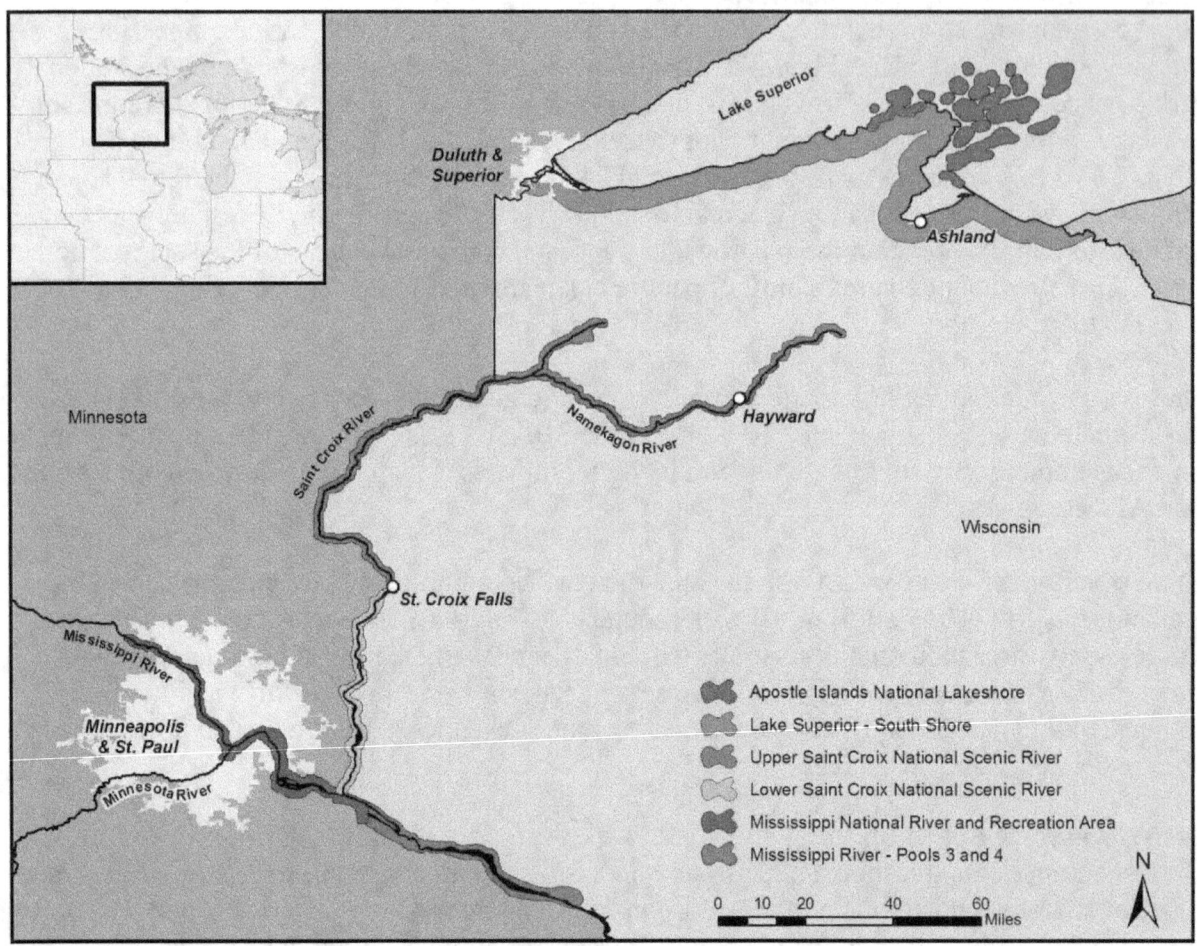

Figure 1. Map of six study areas where bald eagle nestlings were sampled for environmental contaminants, 2006 through 2009.

Mississippi National River and Recreation Area
The Mississippi National River and Recreation Area (MISS or Recreation Area) includes 123 km (77 mi) of the Mississippi River (including navigation pools 1, 2, and the upper 1/3 of pool 3) and 6.4 km (4 mi) of the Minnesota River flowing through the Twin Cities of Minneapolis and St. Paul, Minnesota (Figure 1). The area also includes a short section of the Vermillion River and smaller perennial tributary streams and backwater sloughs. The St. Croix confluence occurs 7.7 km upstream of the MISS outlet boundary. The Recreation Area encompasses 21,853 ha (54,000 acres) of public and private land and water, though <25 ha (60 acres) are owned by the NPS.

The MISS corridor is used primarily by residents of the metropolitan Twin Cities. In 2006, the seven-county Twin Cities Metropolitan area had a population of 2.8 million and U.S. census data from 2005 showed 1,302 people / mi^2 (500 / km^2) in the 701 mi^2 (1,816 km^2) area that includes 42 zip codes immediately adjacent to MISS.

This section of the Mississippi River is a major transportation corridor with use ranging from small pleasure craft to large barges. The area immediately surrounding the river is residential in the north, becoming more urban and industrialized centrally, and then turning rural after leaving the Twin Cities. The metropolitan Twin Cities contributes airborne pollutants, direct waste streams from industrial and public disposal systems, and urban runoff. There are 114 hazardous waste sites within or near MISS; 19 are on Minnesota's Superfund list and six are on the national Superfund list. Moraska-Lafrancois and Glase (2005) reported 98 industrial dischargers within three miles (4.8 km) of MISS. Moreover, 60% of the nearly 485,623 ha (1,875 mi^2) in the Upper Mississippi River floodplain are now used for crop and pastureland (USGS 2010). Erosion in the basin exceeds the rate of soil formation, resulting in a net increase of sediments entering the Mississippi River. The sediments increase turbidity, carry excessive nutrients into the aquatic ecosystem, and are associated with pesticides and other toxic chemicals.

St. Croix National Scenic Riverway

The St. Croix National Scenic Riverway (SACN or Riverway) encompasses 37,528 ha (145 mi^2) including 405 km (252 miles) of the St. Croix and Namekagon Rivers in eastern Minnesota and northwest Wisconsin (Figure 1). The entire St. Croix River watershed covers approximately 2 million ha (7,760 mi^2), which transitions from forest and wetland-dominated lands in the north to more urban and agriculture areas in the south. Wetlands are common throughout the region, but encompass a much greater percent of the contributing drainage area in the upper St. Croix and Namekagon Rivers than in the lower sections of the St. Croix.

The Riverway is divided into two distinct management zones: the lower St. Croix River (L-SACN), and the upper St. Croix and Namekagon Rivers (U-SACN). We used these management zones to subdivide the Riverway into two study areas with the hydroelectric dam at St. Croix Falls, Wisconsin, as the boundary between upper and lower SACN (Figure 1). These study areas differ ecologically and in patterns of human land-use (Magdalene et al.2008). Anthropogenic land use ranges from 2-32% in the upper SACN to >60% along the lower SACN (Wan et al. 2007). U.S. census data from 2005 shows 25 people / mi^2 in the 3,315 mi^2 area including 18 zip codes adjacent to the upper SACN and 181 people / mi^2 in 868 mi^2 in 17 zip codes adjacent to the lower SACN. The lower river and upper portions of the Riverway also differ in their groundwater source (Wan et al. 2007). Moreover, water levels are naturally flowing in the upper section of the Riverway whereas the lower St. Croix is regulated by a hydroelectric dam at St. Croix Falls.

The NPS estimates about 480,000 visitors come to the Riverway annually and much of that use occurs in the lower sections of the river. Urban sprawl from Minneapolis and St. Paul greatly affects river use and pollution of the lower river. Moraska-Lafrancois and Glase (2005) report 41 industrial dischargers within three miles (4.8 km) of SACN, many which occur in the lower river. Numerous private, state, county, and other federal landowners along the corridor complicate the management of resource use. As a result of these pressures, American Rivers, an organization dedicated to preserving free-flowing rivers, declared the lower St. Croix as one of America's most endangered rivers in 2009. Nonetheless, water quality is currently considered excellent and the St. Croix and Namekagon Rivers are listed as "Outstanding" and "Exceptional

Water Resources" by the Minnesota and Wisconsin Departments of Natural Resources respectively.

Mississippi River Pools 3 & 4

This section of the Mississippi River is 78 km (48 mi) long, immediately downstream from the MISS study area, and 7.7 km (4.8 mi) downstream from the confluence with the St. Croix River (Figure 1). The study area is named Pools 3 & 4, but it contains the lower two-thirds of Pool 3 and the upper two-thirds of Pool 4 as they are delineated for river navigation. The administrative boundary of the Mississippi National River and Recreation Area (MISS study area) encompasses the upriver one-third of Pool 3, and we ended the downstream portion of the Pools 3 & 4 study area at the southern end of Lake Pepin. The study area is dominated by Lake Pepin, a 103 km^2 (40 mi^2) lake formed by a natural alluvial dam where the Chippewa River flows into the Mississippi. Lake Pepin begins about 80 km (50 mi) downstream from Minneapolis-St. Paul. Two other large lakes above Lake Pepin, Sturgeon Lake and North Lake, are shallow backwaters of the Mississippi River and are surrounded by swamps and lowland forest. Ownership of the land around the Pools 3 & 4 area is a mixture of Tribal (Prairie Island Tribal Community), federal, state, and private. Large cities along the river include Red Wing (population 16,000), Lake City, Minnesota (4,900), and Pepin, Wisconsin (580 in Pepin Township). A half dozen other small communities are scattered along both sides of the river. Potential industrial discharge occurs at Prairie Island Nuclear Facility north of Red Wing and at the city of Red Wing.

Occupancy and Productivity Estimates

Bald eagle nest occupancy was determined during April and May each year by observers in a fixed-wing aircraft, helicopter, or boat. The Wisconsin Department of Natural Resources (WDNR) conducted all fixed-wing occupancy surveys for APIS, SACN, and LSSS. The WDNR has conducted such occupancy surveys since the early 1980s. The Minnesota Department of Natural Resources (MDNR) also has done occupancy surveys for over two decades but discontinued them after 2005. In 2006 we conducted the occupancy survey at MISS by boat; thereafter, the occupancy survey for nests at MISS and Pools 3& 4 were conducted from a helicopter by the Ramsey County Parks Department.

A nest was considered occupied if one of the following criteria was met: an adult was observed on the nest in incubation posture, eggs or young were observed, two adults were observed near an empty nest, or the nest was recently repaired or contained new nest material (e.g., egg cup with fresh lining) even if adult(s) were not observed (Postupalsky 1983). GPS coordinates for all potentially active bald eagle nests were obtained during these occupancy surveys.

Traditionally, aerial occupancy surveys are followed by aerial productivity surveys to document nest success and the number of young produced. Since neither Wisconsin nor Minnesota is now conducting productivity surveys on a regular basis, we based productivity on the number of young present during our ground visit. Occasionally nests were missed during the aerial occupancy survey. These nests were reported by others or were located during our field work. Data from these nests were excluded from productivity calculations as inclusion of data from nests found after hatching may cause over-estimation of reproductive rates.

The occupancy and productivity surveys provided two critical measures of bald eagle productivity: 1) the percent of occupied nests (we use nest and territory synonymously because a pair of bald eagles will have only one active nest in their territory each year) that were successful (number of nests with at least one young / the number of occupied nests), and 2) the number of young per occupied nest (number of young / number of occupied nests).

Sample Collections and Handling

From mid May through early June each year, when eaglets were between five and nine weeks old, we attempted to climb to each nest and bring the eaglets to the ground for sampling. Nests were excluded if they were extremely difficult to access, if they were unsafe to climb (e.g., in a dead tree or with unstable nest structure), or if the landowner denied access. Nests in only two areas were excluded due to difficulty with access: one in the upper SACN and one in the lower MISS). Both nest trees were in large expanses of bog/marsh that would have required more time and effort than we could allocate to single nests. Occasionally, nests were left un-sampled when young were too old to safely handle or if inclement weather precluded sampling.

All safe, accessible nests were climbed using either traditional spur climbing methods (~80% of 2006 nests) or soft-climbing techniques (~20% of 2006 nests and all nests thereafter). Soft-climbing involved use of a cross bow to shoot a fly-fishing line over a branch near the nest. The fly-line was used to pull a larger cord and then a climbing rope over the branch. The climbing rope was then anchored to the base of a tree and its free-end climbed with mechanical ascenders.

Climbers hand-captured young eaglets in the nest and brought eaglets to the ground in individual handling bags. Handling bags were made of rip-stop nylon with double bottoms and draw-cord openings for safe handling of the nestlings. Once on the ground, nestlings were examined for general health and abnormalities before being weighed, measured, banded, and sampled for environmental contaminants. Weight was determined to the nearest 0.5 kg with a spring scale; measurements (nearest 1 mm) were done with a metal ruler or calipers and included footpad length (between points of talon insertion of the hallux and the front middle toe), length of the 6th and/or 8th primary, and length and depth of the beak. In 2006 we measured the 6th primary, in 2007 both 6th and 8th were measured [R^2 = .99], and thereafter only the 8th was measured. Length of the 8th primary was used in combination with the eaglets sex to determine age in days following methods of Bortolotti (1984). All measurements followed methods described by Bortolotti (1984), and previously used by Bowerman (1993), Dykstra et al. (2005), and others.

We took ≤11 mL of blood to determine concentrations of the organic compounds DDT, DDE, DDD, PCBs, PBDEs, and PFCs. Blood was drawn from the brachial vein with a sterile, 10-cc polypropylene syringe, and 20-gauge needle. The blood sample was immediately transferred to a 10-cc, green-top vacutainer containing sodium heparin to prevent clotting. The small amount of blood remaining in the syringe was forced on to a small square (5-10 cm) of cotton gauze. This blot was later sent to a genetics laboratory to determine the nestling's gender. Three to four breast feathers were plucked from each nestling for determining concentrations of total mercury (THg) and lead (Pb). All samples were individually marked, dated, and placed in a cooler on blue ice until they were processed at the end of each field day.

Within 12 hours of collection, blood samples were spun at 1200 rpm in a centrifuge for 10-12 minutes to separate plasma from the red blood cells. A sterile glass pipette was used to draw-off the plasma into separate vials. One-half (0.5) or 1.0 mL of plasma was placed in a polypropylene vial for PFC determinations and the remaining plasma (4-6 mL) placed in a glass vial for the other organic chemicals. Glass pipettes and vials had been previously baked at 650°F (343°C) to remove chemical residue; polypropylene vials were verified by a second laboratory (see below) as being free of PFC contamination. All vials with plasma and red blood cells were immediately frozen and kept frozen until delivered to an analytical laboratory.

Blood and feather samples were taken from all siblings in a nest; however, samples from only one nestling was submitted to the Wisconsin State Laboratory of Hygiene (WSLH) in Madison, Wisconsin, to quantify target contaminants. Samples from the remaining siblings were archived at WSLH (serum in freezers at -20 °C; feathers dried in envelopes) for future analyses.

For PFCs we split samples for blind comparisons with two other laboratories. A small amount of plasma (~0.5 ml) remaining from the WSLH analysis in 2006 and 2007 were provided to the USEPA analytical laboratory at Research Triangle Park, NC for analysis. In 2008 we split all plasma samples for PFCs each day and submitted frozen samples to both WSLH and USEPA. In 2009 we broadened this laboratory comparison and split PFC samples three ways and sent 0.5 mL to WSLH, USEPA, and the 3M laboratory in St. Paul, Minnesota. All split samples were blind, in identical vials, and were frozen. Analyses of three sets of all materials used to collect and store PFC sample--including syringes, needles, vacutainers, and vials--by the 3M laboratory verified that these materials were free of PFC contamination. Analyses from all three laboratories were not available at the time of this writing and will be reported in a future issue of this technical report series.

Laboratory Analyses and Quality Assurance

All contaminant concentrations reported here were analyzed by the Wisconsin State Laboratory of Hygiene (WSLH) in Madison, Wisconsin. Concentrations of total mercury in feather samples are reported as wet weight (wet wt.) and were determined by cold-vapor atomic absorption spectrophotometry. Lead in feathers are reported as wet weight and determined by flameless atomic absorption spectrophotometry. Plasma concentrations of p,p'-DDT, p,p'-DDE, p,p'-DDD (hereafter DDT, DDE, and DDD), nine PBDE congeners, and 75 PCB congeners were analyzed by gas chromatography/electron capture detection (GC-ECD). PFC analytes in plasma (from 2 to 6 analytes) were determined by high performance liquid chromatography/tandem mass spectrometry (HPLC-MS/MS). For lists of chemical names and congeners, see Appendix A.

The WSLH limits of detection (LOD) varied by analyte, ranging from 0.004 ug/g for mercury to 6.0 ug/L for PCB congener #003 (Appendix C). For quality assurance WSLH added matrix spikes for each batch of 10 plasma samples. Matrix spikes consisted of a known quantity of all target compounds added to chicken serum as a check on the laboratory's ability to efficiently recover the target compounds. In addition, surrogate spikes were added to each sample to assess the extraction process. PCB congeners #14, #65, and #166 were used for surrogate spikes because of their similarity to the targeted compounds and their general absence in our eaglet samples. Surrogate spikes were used to verify that the extraction, clean-up, and concentration steps were performed correctly for each specific sample. Acceptable recoveries were determined by statistical analysis of multiple spikes and varied among compounds.

Lab measurements were reported as concentrations and coded as to quality. Codes included the following: good value with no problems, value below the laboratory's limit of detection (LOD) or report limit (RL) hereafter combined as LOD, interference with another chemical, calibration curve exceeded, above LOD but below limit of quantification (LOQ), problems with laboratory blank, and concentration estimated (results outside of the LOQ but an estimate was possible). We summarized data results for each compound or congener as the percentage of observations that were below the LOD (censored), or for which a measured concentration was considered quantifiable (uncensored). Compounds tended to fall into three groups: 1) those that resulted in measured concentrations all or most of the time (mercury, DDE, some analytes of PFCs, PBDEs, and PCBs), 2) those that were below the LOD most of the time (DDT, some analytes of PFCs, PBDEs, and PCBs), and 3) those that had measurable concentrations in intermediate numbers of samples (lead and DDD).

For comparisons among study areas with mixed effects models (see below) we used only results for analytes that were above the LOD in ≥80% of the samples, except for PCB congeners, which we used only if above the LOD in ≥90% of the samples. We also excluded PFC analytes when the percent recovery of matrix spikes differed from the known concentration by more than 20%. We did not, however, exclude PCB and PBDE congeners that had recovery rates beyond this 20% cutoff. This is because past investigators in our study area, using the same laboratory for both PCBs and PBDEs, have not excluded such analytical data and we wanted to keep our information comparable. Only one PBDE congener (#138) failed this criterion and in only one year (2009). Several PCB congeners failed this criterion, but usually they were within 30%, which many QA/QC programs (e.g., Minnesota Department of Health) feel is acceptable.

Analytes that met our criteria were DDE, mercury, five congeners of PBDEs (47, 99, 100, 153, and 154), 10 PFC analytes (PFDA, PFDS, PFHpS, PFHxS, PFNA, PFOA, PFOS, PFTeDA, PFTrDA, and PFuDA), and 15 congeners of PCBs (178, 180, 183, 185, 187/182, 193, 194, 198, 199, 201, 202/171, 203/196, 206, 207, and 208/195). Of these, only two were below the LOD in more than 10% of our samples (PBDE congeners 153 and 154). For analytes that met our criteria, but where samples were below the LOD, we used ½ the LOD as the estimated concentration in calculations except for PCBs where we used zero (see PCB result section for a comparison of both non-parametric and parametric techniques).

Many of the contaminants not used in the mixed effects models were detected only rarely, yet when detected, the location and level of contamination is important. It is also important to know where contaminants were tested but not found. For these reasons, we included all measured values and non-detections on distribution maps.

Statistical Analysis

Data sets that include observations below the LOD present special problems for quantitative analysis. Three methods of analysis of such data are possible: one is substitution, which involves replacing all censored observations with one value, such as 0, ½ the LOD, or the LOD itself; the second is maximum likelihood analysis in which the data are assumed to follow a specified distribution; and the third is nonparametric analysis in which ranking methods are used to estimate values and compare groups (Helsel 2005). For analytes that consisted mostly of censored observations we did no statistical analyses. Because many of these were below the

LOD in more than 50% of the samples, it was not possible to estimate the median concentration. Most of the remaining compounds and congeners had either no censored observations or very few (usually less than 10%). For these analytes we used the simple substitution procedure, with ½ the LOD as the value. The one situation for which we did not use the substitution method was summing up total PCBs across the 75 measured congeners. In this case we used a nonparametric method suggested by Helsel (2009) to handle observations below the detection limit when summing across congeners to compute total PCBs. We also compared this method with the simpler method of replacing observations below the detection limit by zero when computing total PCBs, as a comparison with previous work on PCBs in bald eagles (Dykstra et al. 2005) The nonparametric method is most effective when congeners have different LODs, which is the case for PCBs (eight different LODs; Helsel 2009).

All concentrations were log transformed before analysis. Most of the analytes exhibited skewed distributions with a long upper tail (a few high concentrations), suggesting better symmetry on the log scale. Environmental contaminants are often lognormally distributed because they arise from random dilution processes (Ott 1995). We examined standard plots of residuals from all analyses to assess whether model assumptions were satisfied.

For comparisons of contaminant levels among regions, we analyzed the data with mixed effects models that included territory as a random effect and region as a fixed effect. These models can account for the potential lack of independence among observations from the same territories. Samples collected from the same territory in different years are likely not independent because the territories are often occupied by the same adults for several years and the environmental characteristics of the territories, including the forage base, remain relatively constant over time. The Tukey-Kramer method was used for pair-wise comparisons among regions.

We also examined the effect of eaglet age (days) and weight (kg) on concentrations of contaminants. Age and weight did not have a significant effect on contaminant concentrations for mercury, DDE, or for any congeners of PCBs or PBDEs, but they did have a significant effect for some PFC analytes. To account for this, we included age or weight as covariates in mixed effects models with study area as a fixed effect and territory as a random effect.

For statistical comparisons between study areas, the means of log-transformed values were estimated from the mixed effects models, which account for the random effects in the model and thus for differing numbers of observations for each territory (Searle 1987). These estimated regional means are very similar to means computed by averaging first over all observations within a territory, and then averaging over the territory means in each region. Geometric means were computed by back-transforming the means of the log-transformed observations. A Type I error (α) of 0.05 was used to judge the significance of statistical tests.

For simplicity in reporting annual tabular summaries we calculated geometric means directly from the data, not from the random effects models. These values were back transformed to the original scale and the resulting geometric means are very close to those estimated from the mixed effects models.

Results

Productivity and Mortality

Productivity across the four years ranged from a low of 1.0 young/occupied nest at APIS to 2.2 young/occupied nest at MISS (Figure 2, Table 1). Similarly, the percent of occupied nests that were successful ranged from 63% at APIS to 100% at MISS. Annual productivity and nest success estimates varied by year and study area, but in all years where data were available nest success and productivity met or exceeded the criteria of $\geq$50% nest success and $\geq$1.0 young/occupied nest, which is considered necessary for a healthy bald eagle population (Wiemeyer et al. 1984, Bowerman 2003).

Sample size in some years was small due to few active territories or no data collection. Pools 3&4 and LSSS study areas were not part of the NPS's normal monitoring activities, and data were obtained only when outside funding was available. Further, due to budget constraints WDNR did not conduct productivity flights in 2009 (occupancy only) and in accordance with our protocol we did not sample at U-SACN in 2008, or at APIS and U-SACN in 2009. We believe aerial surveys to locate occupied nests for the L-SACN were inadequate in three of the four years (2006, 2007, and 2009); in 2008 we augmented flight data with ground observations and the estimated number of occupied nests increased because of that effort.

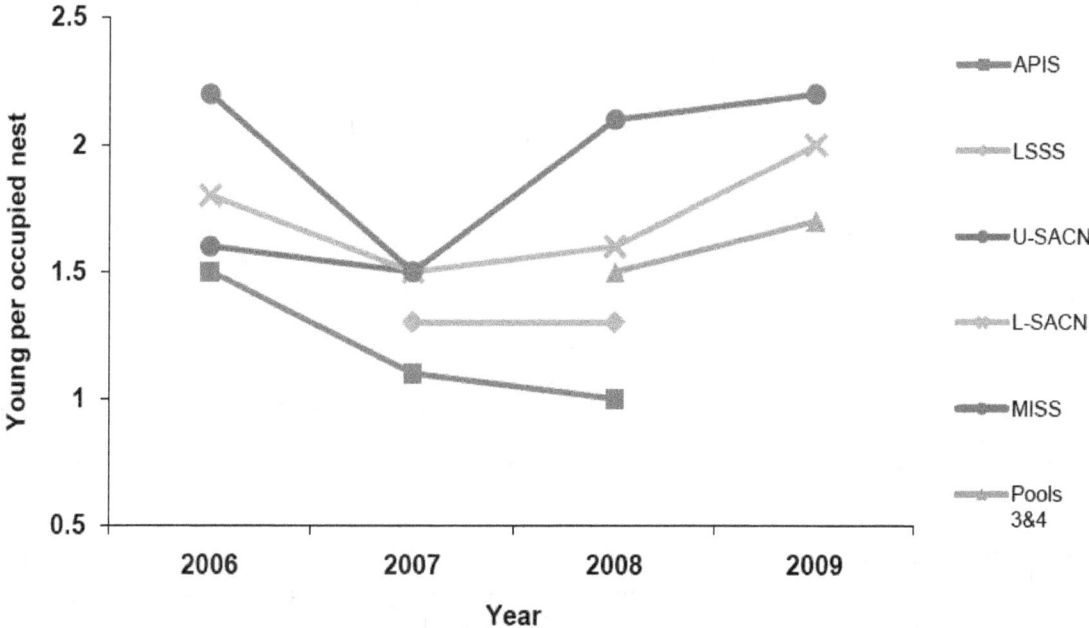

Figure 2. Number of young per occupied bald eagle nest for six study areas.

Table 1. Number of nests occupied, percent nest success, and number of young produced per occupied nest for bald eagles in six study areas, 2006-2009. Data are from the Wisconsin Department of Natural Resources and this study. ND = no data available.

Study area / parameter	Year				
	2006	2007	2008	2009	Avg
APIS					
# occupied nests [a]	12(11)	9	8	12	10
% successful	91%	67%	63%	ND	74%
young / occupied nest	1.5	1.1	1.0	ND	1.2
LSSS					
# occupied nests [a]	16	14	24(4)	15	17
% successful	63%	79%	100%*	ND	81%
young / occupied nest	1.1	1.3	1.3*	ND	1.2
U-SACN					
# occupied nests [a]	20	20(19)	17	18	19
% successful	90%	79%	ND	ND	85%
young / occupied nest	1.6	1.5	ND	ND	1.6
L-SACN					
# occupied nests [a]	5	5(4)	13(10)	5(4)	7*
% successful	80%*	100%*	70%	100%*	88%*
young / occupied nest	1.8*	1.5*	1.6	2.0*	1.7*
MISS					
# occupied nests [a]	13(11)	20(15)	20(14)	28(20)	20
% successful	91%	80%	100%	95%	92%
young / occupied nest	2.2	1.5	2.1	2.2	2.0
Pools 3&4					
# occupied nests [a]	ND	ND	30(24)	15(12)	23
% successful	ND	ND	88%	83%	86%
young / occupied nest	ND	ND	1.5	1.7	1.6

[a] = Number of occupied nests in the study area as determined by aerial flights and ground observations; number in parentheses was used for % occupancy and productivity calculations in cases where one or more nests were not examined for productivity.
* = Based on a small sample, estimate should be used with caution.

We occasionally found addled eggs or dead eaglets in the nest and dead eaglets on the ground under the nest. Addled eggs were collected and frozen for later analysis. Cause of death was determined for five eaglets; others could not be determined due to advanced stages of decay (Table 2). Two eaglets were found dead in the water in 2006 when their nest blew down along the Mississippi River. These two specimens were donated to the Bell Museum of Minnesota. In 2007 we collected one dead eaglet from its nest on Pig's Eye Lake on the Mississippi River. The University of Minnesota, Veterinary Diagnostics Laboratory established cause of death as *Pasteurella multocida* septicemia – a bacterium associated with waterfowl and sometimes transmitted to predators. In 2008 an injured eaglet was found in a nest on the south shore of Lake Superior with treble hooks from a fishing lure deeply embedded in its leg and monofilament line wrapped tightly around the leg and anchored to the nest. The eaglet was transported to the Raptor Center at the University of Minnesota where it was euthanized after finding the leg was broken and unrepairable. One eaglet died in 2009 when it stepped off the nest as we approached it for handling; this was our only study-related mortality (0.3% of birds handled).

We did not search for addled eggs in 2006. Bald eagles tend to add nest material on top of addled eggs and beginning in 2007 all nests were examined. A total of nine addled eggs were collected in a three year period; causes of addling were unknown and laboratory analysis for egg-shell thinning and contaminant levels in these eggs is pending (Table 2).

Table 2. Causes of mortality for bald eagle nestlings found, proportion of young found dead, and number of addled eggs found during routine banding and sampling activities; ND = no data.

	Year			
Cause of death	**2006**	**2007**	**2008**	**2009**
Unknown	2	2		
Nest fell	2			
Fishing line			1	
Disease		1		
Study-related				1
Total found dead	4	3	1	1
Total found alive	80	91	98	95
% found dead	4.8	3.2	1.0	1.1
Addled eggs found	ND	2	4	3

Eaglet Sampling

We obtained feather and plasma samples from at least one nestling from each active nest to determine levels of target contaminants. We visited from 34 to 46 nests each year and measured, banded, and sampled a total of 288 nestling bald eagles (Table 3). Female nestlings were slightly larger than males, and age and sex ratios varied across study areas (Table 4). The overall sex ratio was near parity (94:100) though it differed in some years due to small sample sizes.

Occasionally the feather or blood sample was not obtained due to the young age of the nestling or other circumstances (e.g., very young nestlings lack breast feathers and blood samples could not be obtained from some nestlings). Of the 288 nestlings handled, we sent 142 feather and 154 blood samples to the WSLH for contaminant analysis. Annual sample size for each study area depended on the number of active nests and ranged from as few as five at L-SACN to as many as 40 at MISS. We also sent 166 plasma samples for inter-laboratory comparisons of PFCs (33 in 2006, 35 in 2007, 61 in 2008, and 37 in 2009). Data from the inter-laboratory comparisons are not yet available.

Unanalyzed samples (121 feather and 123 plasma) from siblings were archived at WSLH (Table 3).

Table 3. Number of bald eagle nestlings sampled, tissue samples analyzed, and tissues archived for environmental contaminants. Grey highlighting indicates years and study areas that are part of the routine sampling scheme for long-term monitoring at three national parks; those not highlighted were added with funding and in-kind support from institutional partners.

Study Area	Year	Territories sampled	Young banded	Young sampled	Feather samples analyzed	Feather samples archived	Plasma samples analyzed	Plasma samples archived
APIS	2006	9	10	11	9	2	8	2
	2007	6	10	9	6	3	6	3
	2008	5	8	8	4	3	5	3
LSSS	2007	6	10	10	6	4	6	4
	2008	4	6	5	4	1	4	1
U-SACN	2006	11	17	17	11	6	11	6
	2007	8	14	13	8	5	8	5
L-SACN	2006	3	5	5	3	2	3	2
	2007	4	6	7	4	3	4	2
	2008	7	16	16	7	9	7	9
	2009	9	19	27	9	10	9	14
MISS	2006	11	24	21	11	9	11	7
	2007	11	18	18	11	6	12	5
	2008	15	33	31	14	14	15	15
	2009	18	40	40	18	22	18	22
Pools 3&4	2008	15	29	28	14	12	15	13
	2009	12	23	22	12	10	12	10
Totals		154	288	288	142	121	154	123

Table 4. Age, weight, and sex ratios for bald eagle nestlings sampled for environmental contaminants at six study areas, 2006-2009.

Study area	Mean age in days (range; sample)	Average weight in kg (range; sample)		Sex ratio (male: female)
		Males	Females	
APIS	39 (26-52; n=28)	3.30 (2.5-4.0; n=14)	3.85 (2.2-4.7; n=13)	108:100
LSSS	52 (36-69; n=15)	3.47 (3.1-4.1; n=6)	4.55 (3.6-5.2; n=9)	67:100
U-SACN	45 (29-65; n=30)	3.42 (2.5-4.9; n=18)	4.41 (3.5-5.6; n=12)	150:100
L-SACN	41 (26-72; n=44)	3.15 (2.1-3.9; n=21)	4.00 (3.1-4.9; n=21)	100:100
MISS	37 (24-70; n=108)	2.99 (2.1-4.1; n=49)	3.68 (2.1-5.1; n=56)	88:100
Pools 3+4	36 (22-48; n=49)	2.82 (2.0-3.6; n=22)	3.69 (2.2-4.8; n=28)	79:100
Totals	42 (22-72; n=274)	3.19 (2.0-4.9; n=130)	4.03 (2.1-5.6; n=139)	94:100

Contaminant Levels and Spatial Patterns

Heavy Metals

<u>Mercury</u>
Mercury concentrations in breast feathers differed among study areas with significantly higher means at U-SACN, LSSS, and L-SACN than at APIS, MISS, and Pools 3&4 (mixed effects model $P<0.001$; Figure 3). These spatial patterns are striking when maximum levels for each nest are mapped across the four years (Figure 4). Higher levels of mercury were often found along the upper St Croix River and portions of the Lake Superior shoreline where extensive wetlands likely contribute to the microbial production of methyl mercury and its entry into aquatic food webs (Hurley et al. 1995). The lower St. Croix has fewer contributing wetlands but a few nests had high levels, which when combined with a small sample of nests, put L-SACN in the higher category of mercury contamination. Annual levels of mercury varied most at U-SACN and LSSS (Table 5; Appendix D). Concentrations in feather samples from the U-SACN and LSSS study areas declined by 29% and 35% respectively from 2006 to 2007, whereas MISS decreased by 16% and APIS increased by 11% in that same period. We did not explore annual trends with only four years of data; however, our data for APIS and LSSS were combined with data from previous studies by Dykstra et al. (2005) and together they show mercury has declined in eaglets from Lake Superior at a rate of 2.4% per year from 1991 through 2008 (Dykstra et al. 2010).

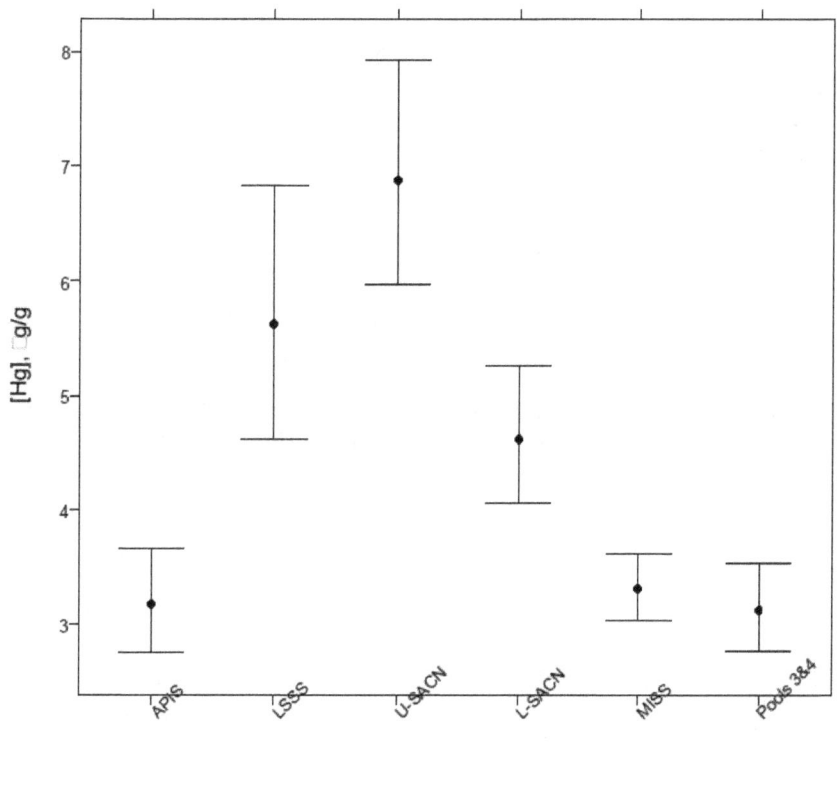

Figure 3. Estimated geometric mean concentrations and 95% confidence intervals (CI) for mercury (wet weight) in bald eagle nestling feathers from six study areas, 2006-2009. Means and CIs are estimated from mixed effects models.

17

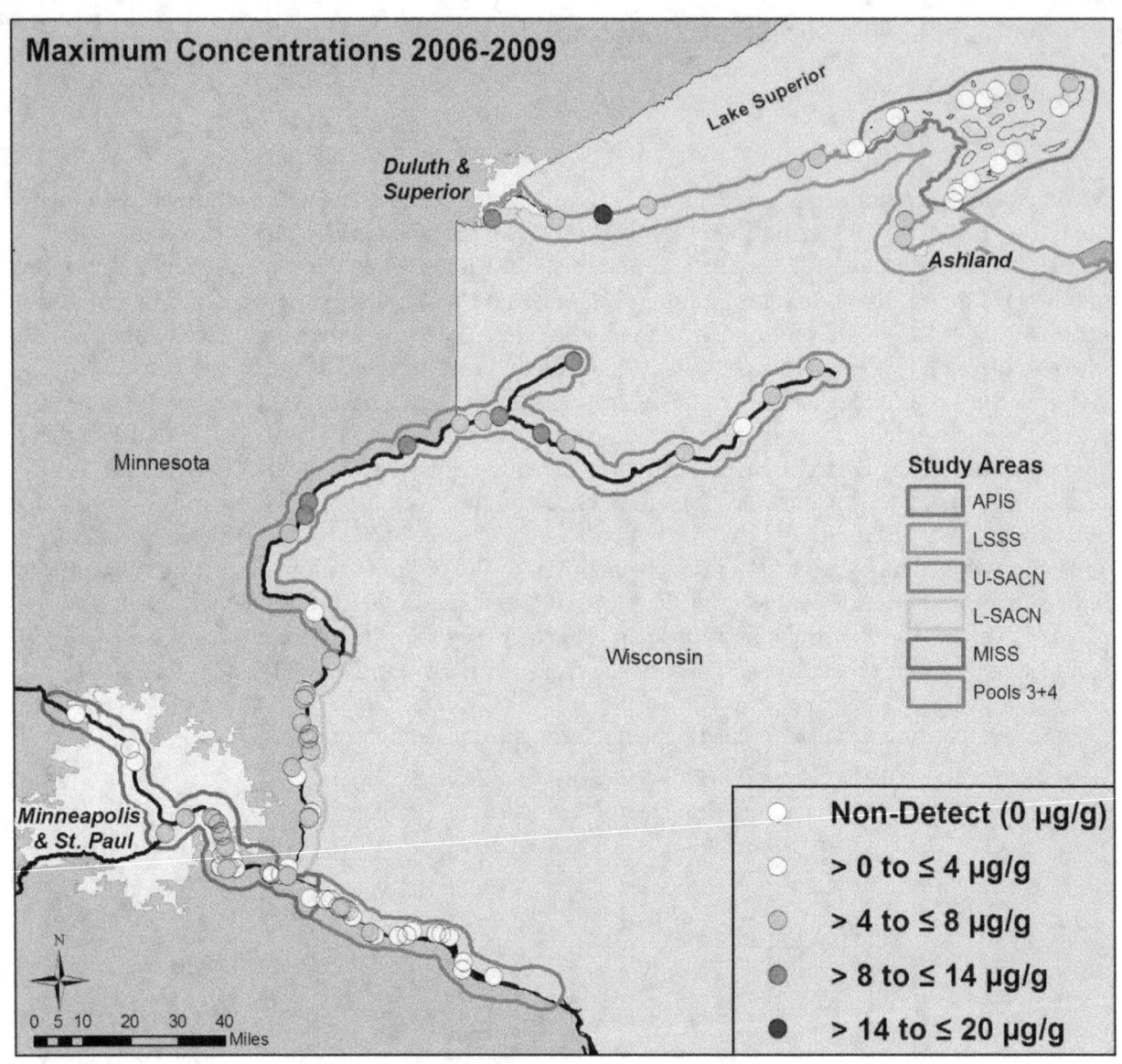

Figure 4. Maximum wet weight concentrations of mercury in breast feathers of bald eagle nestlings from all nests sampled across six study areas, 2006-2009. There were no non-detections.

Table 5. Sample size, measures of central tendency, and variability of total mercury (*ug*/g wet wt.) in breast feathers of bald eagle nestlings, 2006-2009. To calculate summary statistics we used ½ the LOD for samples below the laboratory's limit of detection. See text for study area names.

Study Area	Year	N	Arithmetic				Geometric		
			Mean	Median	SD	SE	Mean	Upper 95% CI	Lower 95% CI
APIS	2006	9	3.26	3.70	1.04	0.35	3.02	4.09	2.24
	2007	6	3.78	3.20	2.14	0.87	3.40	4.99	2.32
	2008	4	3.40	3.15	0.88	0.44	3.32	4.23	2.61
LSSS	2007	6	7.48	5.85	4.45	1.82	6.66	9.93	4.47
	2008	4	4.38	4.40	0.70	0.35	4.33	5.09	3.69
U-SACN	2006	11	8.25	8.30	2.44	0.74	7.96	9.38	6.76
	2007	8	5.89	6.35	1.63	0.58	5.65	7.06	4.53
L-SACN	2006	3	6.20	5.70	1.51	0.87	6.08	7.94	4.66
	2007	4	4.05	4.25	0.76	0.38	3.99	4.87	3.27
	2008	7	4.40	3.80	1.17	0.44	4.28	5.12	3.58
	2009	9	4.86	4.90	0.93	0.31	4.77	5.43	4.19
MISS	2006	11	3.76	3.70	0.73	0.22	3.70	4.16	3.28
	2007	11	3.31	2.80	1.34	0.40	3.12	3.81	2.56
	2008	14	3.46	3.55	0.97	0.26	3.33	3.89	2.85
	2009	18	3.24	3.30	0.52	0.12	3.20	3.45	2.96
Pools 3+4	2008	14	2.76	2.65	0.67	0.18	2.69	3.05	2.38
	2009	12	3.83	3.60	0.89	0.26	3.74	4.22	3.32

Lead

Concentrations of lead in breast feathers exceeded the laboratory's detection limits in 75.5% of the samples, which was fewer than our criteria of $\geq$80% for assessing statistical differences among study areas. Of those above LOD, the measured levels were mostly <1.0 ug/g wet weight across the study areas; though, a few nests around Pig's Eye Lake in MISS, and one nest on the lower SACN had levels exceeding 2.0 ug/g (Table 6, Figure 5). Lead levels were particularly high in 2006 compared to other years for the same study areas. For example, levels at APIS and L-SACN were about five times higher and levels at U-SACN were twice as high in 2006 compared to 2007. This finding is confounded, however, by many samples being non-detections, particularly on Lake Superior (Figure 5).

Table 6. Sample size, measures of central tendency, and variability of lead (ug/g wet wt.) in breast feathers of bald eagle nestlings, 2006-2009. To calculate summary statistics we used ½ the LOD for samples below the laboratories limits of detection. See text for study area names.

| Study Area | Year | N | Arithmetic | | | | Geometric | | |
			Mean	Median	SD	SE	Mean	Upper 95% CI	Lower 95% CI
APIS	2006	9	0.393	0.330	0.205	0.068	0.351	0.487	0.252
	2007	6	0.0700**	0.0700**	0.0000**	0.0000**	0.0700**	0.0700**	0.0700**
	2008	4	0.150	0.110	0.113	0.057	0.123	0.247	0.061
LSSS	2007	6	0.153	0.130	0.095	0.039	0.128	0.219	0.075
	2008	4	0.220	0.155	0.203	0.102	0.156	0.403	0.060
U-SACN	2006	11	0.297	0.340	0.105	0.032	0.277	0.354	0.217
	2007	8	0.159	0.0700	0.1436	0.0508	0.118	0.202	0.069
L-SACN	2006	3	1.28	0.870	1.028	0.594	1.03	2.53	0.42
	2007	4	0.233	0.160	0.210	0.105	0.176	0.403	0.077
	2008	7	0.373	0.280	0.283	0.107	0.279	0.533	0.146
	2009	9	0.172	0.190	0.077	0.026	0.155	0.216	0.111
MISS	2006	11	1.06	0.750	1.008	0.304	0.753	1.244	0.456
	2007	11	0.740	0.400	0.622	0.188	0.567	0.874	0.368
	2008	14	0.341	0.330	0.253	0.068	0.244	0.396	0.150
	2009	18	0.371	0.245	0.526	0.124	0.231	0.351	0.152
Pools 3+4	2008	14	0.201	0.185	0.124	0.033	0.167	0.235	0.119
	2009	12	0.218	0.195	0.135	0.039	0.180	0.263	0.124

**All samples were non-detects.

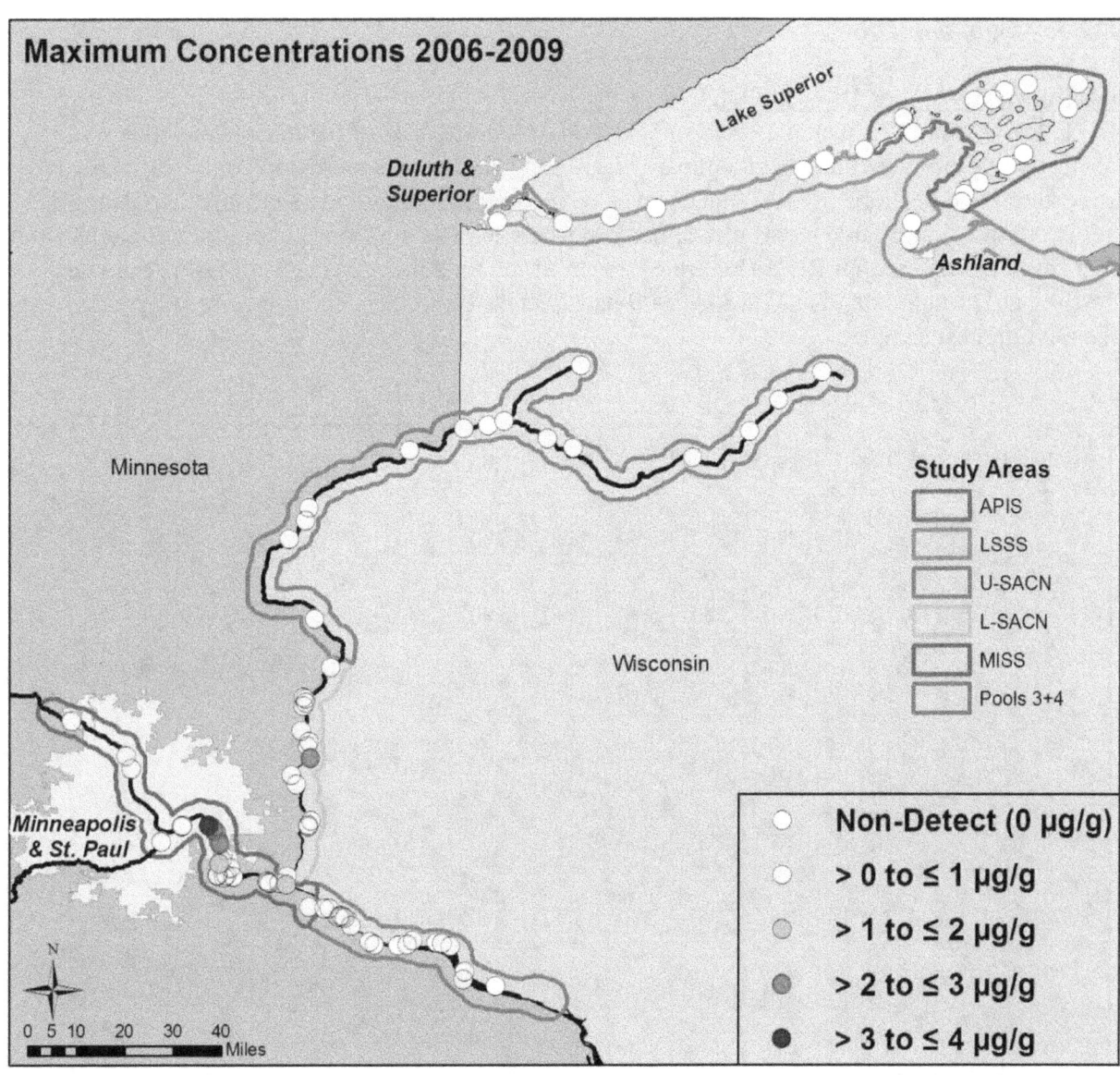

Figure 5. Maximum wet weight concentrations of lead in breast feathers of bald eagle nestlings from all nests sampled across six study areas, 2006-2009.

21

Legacy Contaminants

DDT and Metabolites DDE and DDD

DDT, DDD, and DDE were detected in 5.9%, 74.3%, and 100% of the plasma samples respectively; therefore statistical comparisons among study areas were done only for DDE. We expected few detections of DDT since it was banned more than 30 years prior to our sampling, yet we found quantifiable levels of DDT in nine samples - seven from Lake Superior eaglets and two from the Mississippi River (Figure 6). Eight of the nine had <2.0 ug/L of DDT, but one nestling at Durnam Island at MISS in 2009 had 7.30 ug/L of DDT, about four times greater than the next highest sample.

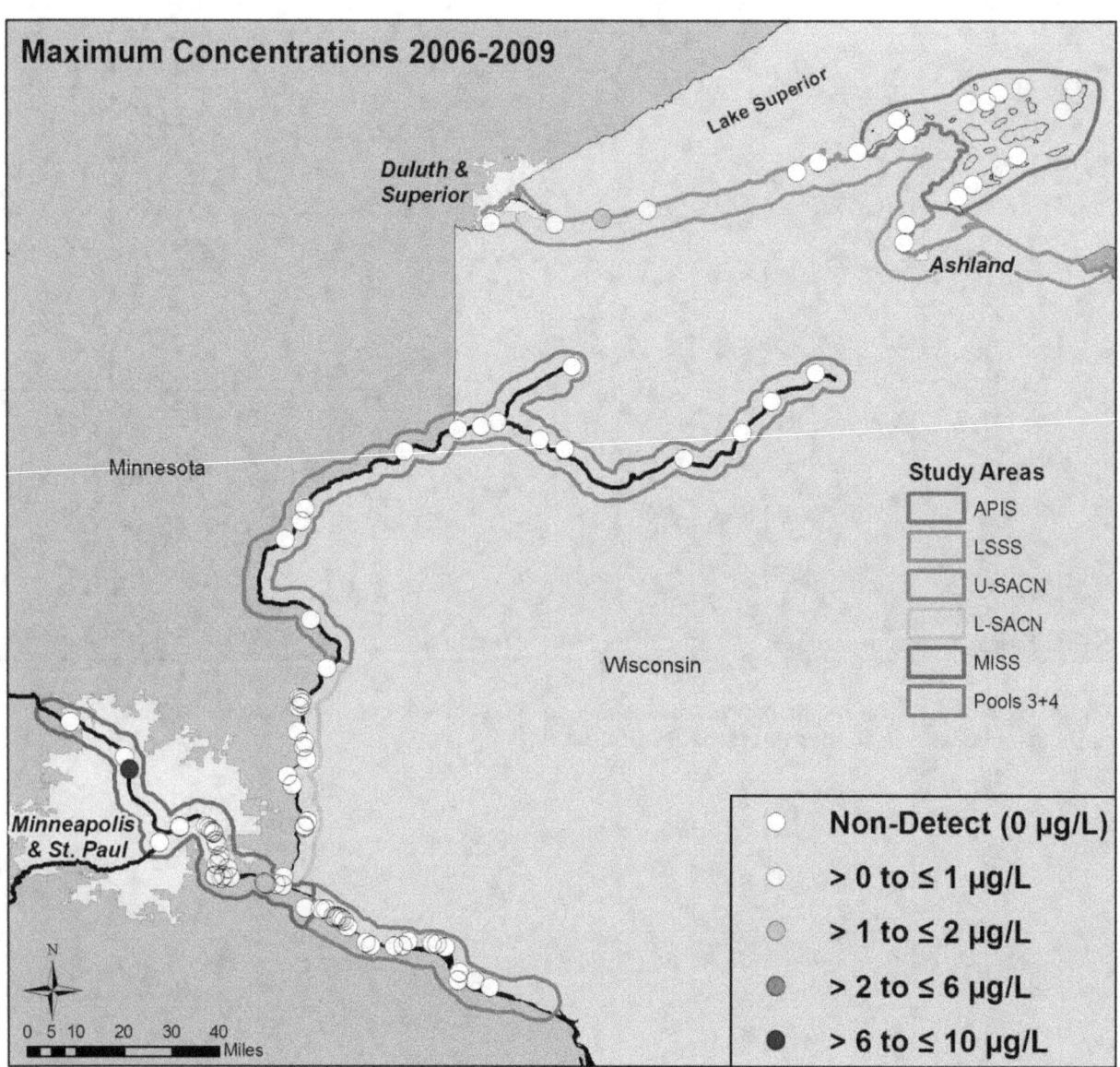

Figure 6. Maximum concentrations of DDT in plasma of bald eagle nestlings from all nests sampled across six study areas, 2006-2009.

DDD and DDE are the breakdown products of DDT and we found these metabolites in plasma from a majority of the nestlings sampled. DDD was detected consistently and found at higher levels in the lower SACN and the Mississippi River study areas compared to the upper SACN, LSSS, and APIS, though this was not tested statistically (Figure 7, Table 7). DDE was found at higher levels than DDD and in all nestlings sampled. This highly persistent metabolite, in contrast to DDD, was found at higher levels at APIS (Figure 8). Differences in the geometric mean concentrations of DDE among study areas were significant ($P<0.001$) with highest levels found in eaglets from APIS; high levels at LSSS (though not significantly different from APIS nor the next lower group); intermediate levels at MISS, L-SACN, and Pools 3&4; and significantly lower at U-SACN (mixed effects model $P<0.001$; Figure 9).

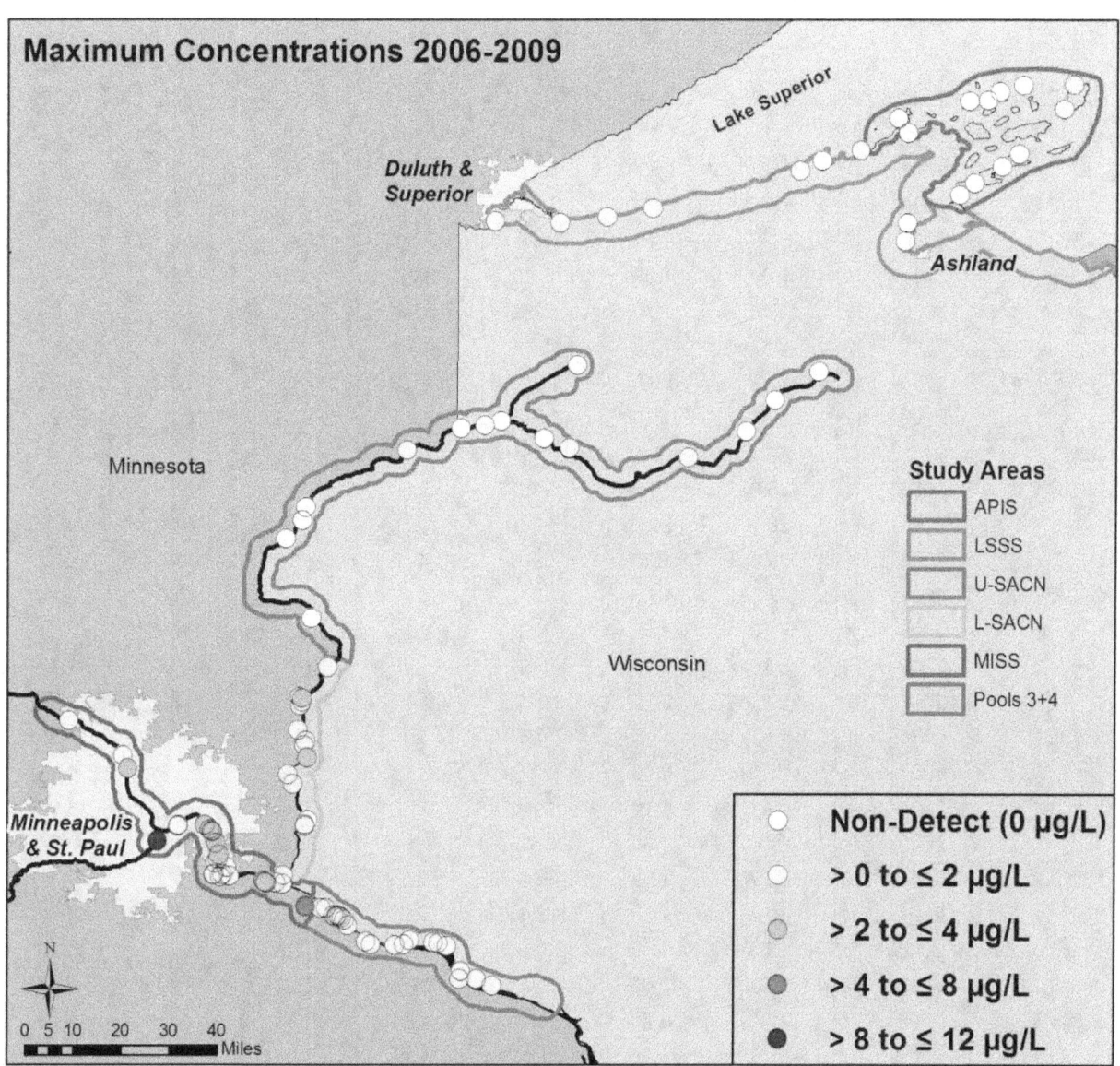

Figure 7. Maximum concentrations of DDD in plasma of bald eagle nestlings from all nests sampled across six study areas, 2006-2009.

23

Table 7. Sample size, measures of central tendency, and variability of DDD and DDE (*ug*/L) in plasma from bald eagle nestlings, 2006-2009. To calculate summary statistics we used ½ the LOD for samples below the laboratories limits of detection. See text for study area names.

| Study Area | Year | N | Arithmetic | | | | Geometric | | |
			Mean	Median	SD	SE	Mean	Upper 95% CI	Lower 95% CI
DDD:									
APIS	2006	8	0.221	0.150	0.133	0.047	0.196	0.275	0.139
	2007	6	0.150**	0.150**	0.000	0.000	0.150**	0.150**	0.150**
	2008	5	0.150**	0.150**	0.000	0.000	0.150**	0.150**	0.150**
LSSS	2007	6	0.563	0.595	0.239	0.098	0.498	0.819	0.303
	2008	4	0.210	0.150	0.120	0.060	0.190	0.304	0.119
U-SACN	2006	11	0.165	0.150	0.048	0.015	0.160	0.182	0.141
	2007	8	0.253	0.150	0.147	0.052	0.220	0.320	0.152
L-SACN	2006	3	1.49	1.10	0.79	0.46	1.37	2.38	0.79
	2007	4	1.16	0.875	0.704	0.352	1.04	1.73	0.62
	2008	7	0.734	0.630	0.310	0.117	0.677	0.939	0.489
	2009	9	0.760	0.660	0.528	0.176	0.571	1.016	0.321
MISS	2006	10	2.28	1.55	1.28	0.40	1.98	2.80	1.40
	2007	11	1.90	1.90	0.90	0.27	1.71	2.28	1.28
	2008	15	2.42	1.70	2.02	0.52	2.03	2.66	1.55
	2009	18	1.37	1.25	0.79	0.19	1.12	1.57	0.80
Pools 3+4	2008	15	1.09	0.990	0.293	0.076	1.05	1.20	0.91
	2009	12	1.08	1.10	0.23	0.07	1.05	1.22	0.91
DDE:									
APIS	2006	8	33.9	28.0	21.6	7.6	29.7	42.4	20.8
	2007	6	29.2	21.0	29.6	12.1	17.7	44.0	7.1
	2008	5	29.3	13.0	29.3	13.1	17.5	49.5	6.2
LSSS	2007	6	17.8	16.5	12.2	5.0	14.7	25.3	8.5
	2008	4	7.70	7.70	3.52	1.76	7.01	11.75	4.18
U-SACN	2006	11	3.78	2.10	4.53	1.37	2.70	4.17	1.75
	2007	8	2.80	2.75	1.12	0.40	2.62	3.43	1.99
L-SACN	2006	3	14.7	11.0	6.4	3.7	13.9	21.8	8.8
	2007	4	7.10	6.00	3.49	1.75	6.54	10.24	4.17
	2008	7	5.81	6.10	2.46	0.93	5.30	7.65	3.67
	2009	9	8.58	7.30	3.42	1.14	8.02	10.32	6.24
MISS	2006	10	12.7	11.5	6.4	2.0	11.5	15.2	8.6
	2007	11	10.9	10.0	3.1	0.9	10.5	12.4	8.9
	2008	15	13.3	11.0	8.9	2.3	11.8	14.8	9.3
	2009	18	7.92	7.50	2.63	0.62	7.52	8.77	6.45
Pools 3+4	2008	15	7.45	6.90	2.71	0.70	6.99	8.45	5.79
	2009	12	8.77	8.15	3.42	0.99	8.34	9.91	7.02

** All samples were non-detects

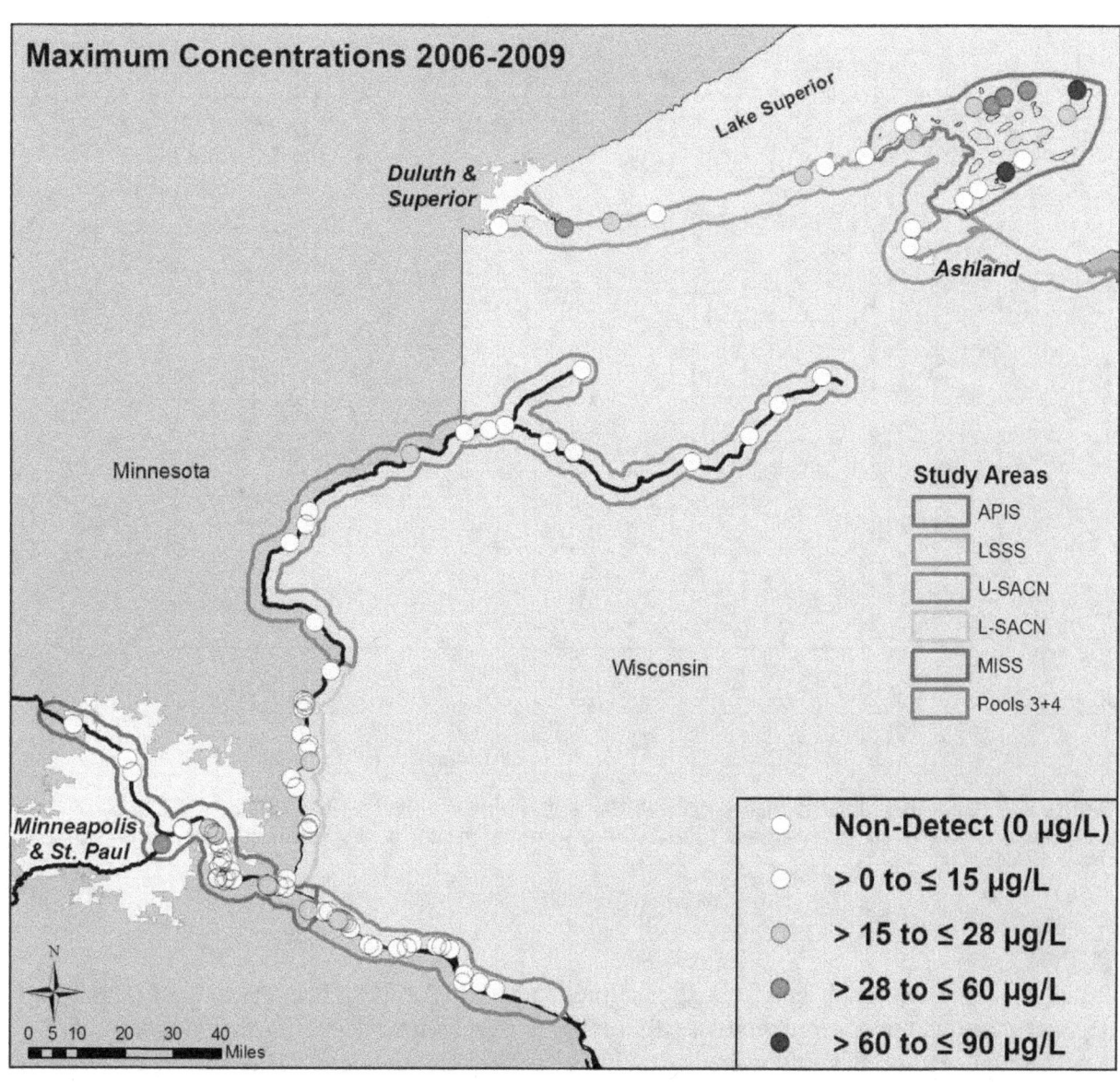

Figure 8. Maximum concentrations of DDE in plasma of bald eagle nestlings from all nests sampled across six study areas, 2006-2009.

Seven nests had nestlings in one or more years with DDE levels at or above 28.0 ug/L in plasma, a threshold concentration for adverse reproductive effects on bald eagle populations (Elliot and Harris 2001/2002). Five of these nests were from APIS and both LSSS and MISS each had one sample above this threshold (Figure 8). However, when combined with data from earlier studies (Dykstra et al. 2005) our data show that DDE has declined in Lake Superior nestlings at a rate of 3% annually from 1989 to 2008 (Dykstra et al. 2010).

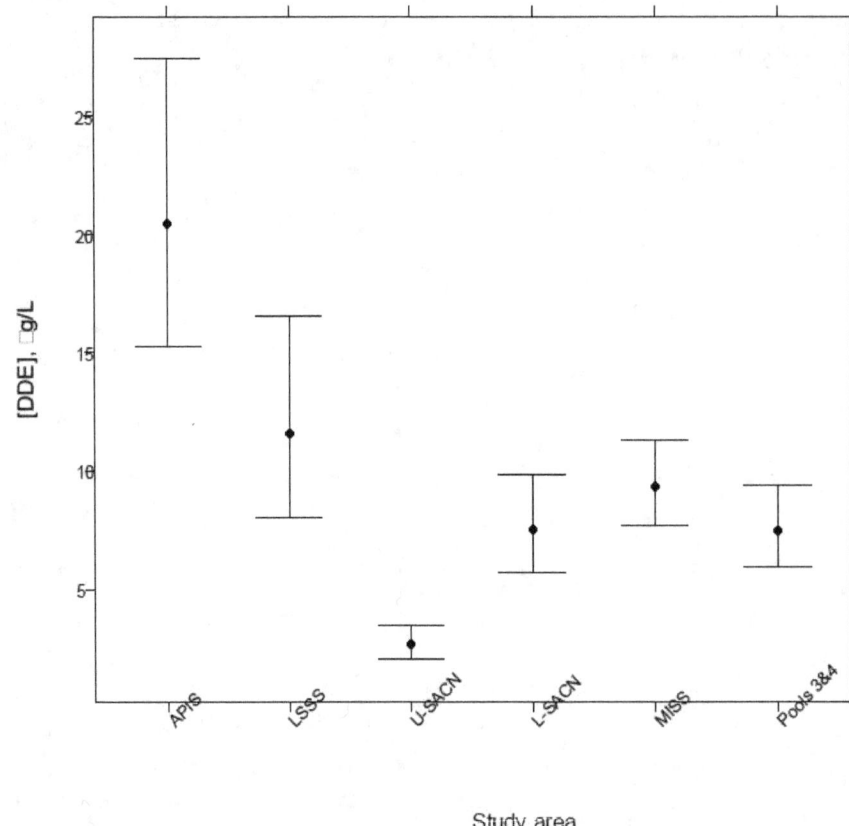

Figure 9. Estimated geometric mean concentrations and 95% confidence intervals for DDE in bald eagle nestlings sampled at six study areas, 2006-2009. Geometric means and confidence intervals calculated from mixed effects models.

PCBs

PCBs were detected in plasma from all nestlings sampled. Total PCB concentrations (sum of all 75 congeners evaluated) were consistently higher in eaglets from L-SACN, MISS and Pools 3 & 4 with some nests on the outer islands of APIS also showing high levels (Figure 10, Table 8). Of the 75 congeners we measured, 15 were detected in ≥80% of the samples and had geometric mean concentrations ranging from 0.10 to 12.7 ug/L (Table 9). There were significant regional differences among these 15 PCB congeners (Table 10). For all congeners, and using either the Kaplan-Meier nonparametric method or with non-detections set at 0, eaglets from U-SACN had the smallest concentrations, usually an order of magnitude lower than other regions (Figure 11, Table 10). Eight of the 15 congeners had their highest concentrations in eaglets from Pools 3 & 4 and these congeners were usually high in L-SACN eaglets also. The remaining seven congeners had their highest concentrations in eaglets from APIS and these congeners were usually higher in LSSS eaglets as well. Total PCBs followed the pattern of highest concentrations in eaglets from Mississippi River and L-SACN study areas, intermediate concentrations in eaglets from APIS and LSSS, and lowest concentrations from the U-SACN (mixed effects model $P<0.001$; Figure 12, Table 10).

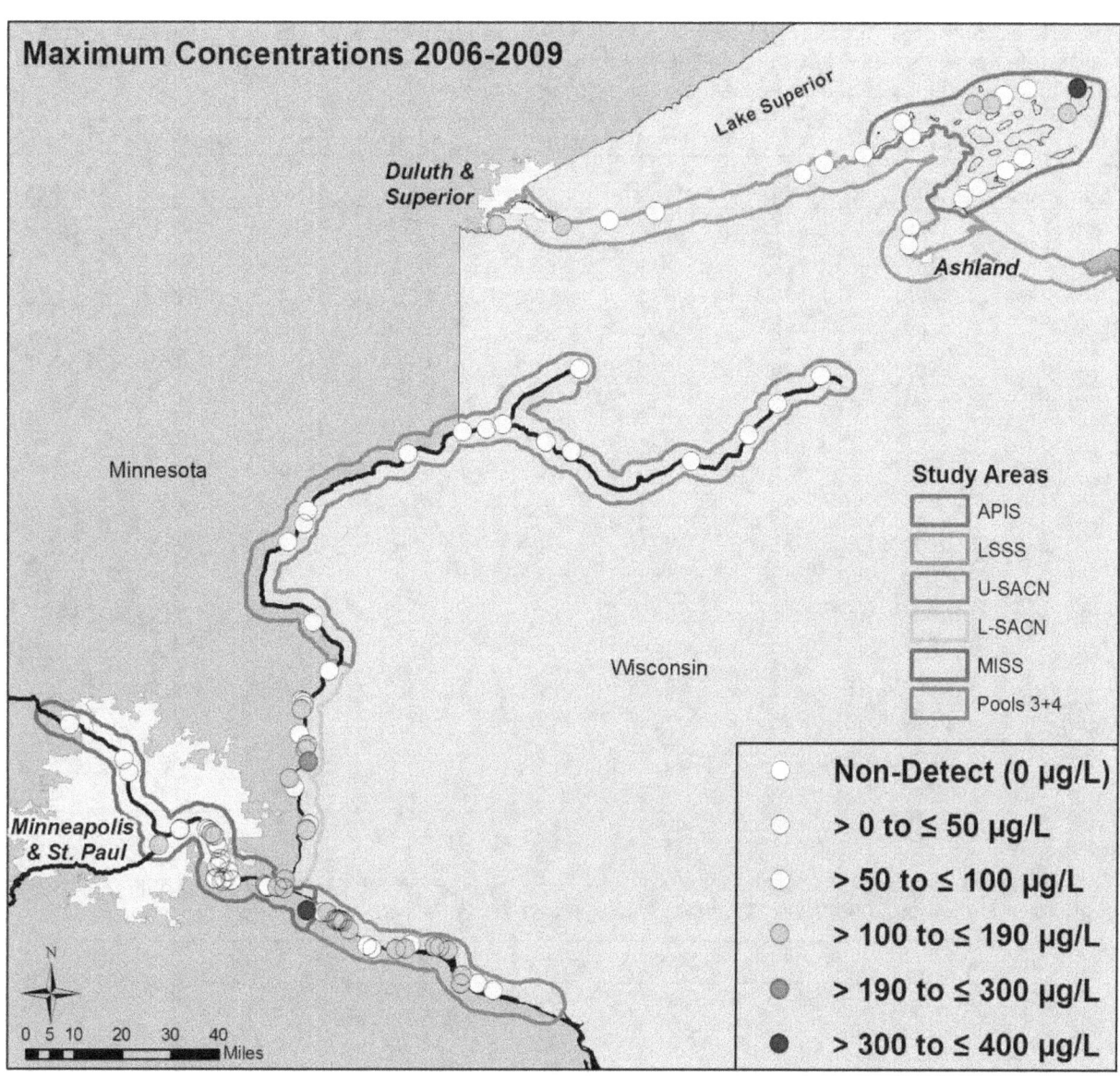

Figure 10. Maximum concentrations of total PCB in plasma of bald eagle nestlings from all nests sampled across six study areas, 2006-2009.

Three nests, one at each of APIS, L-SACN, and MISS, had total PCB levels above 190 ug/L, which is considered the threshold for adverse effects on bald eagle populations (Elliot and Harris 2001/2002). However, our data, combined with data from earlier studies (Dykstra et al. 2005), show that the total PCB load in Lake Superior nestlings has declined at about 4.3% annually from 1989 to 2008 (Dykstra et al. 2010).

Table 8. Sample size, measures of central tendency, and variability of total PCB (*ug*/L) in plasma from bald eagle nestlings, 2006-2009. To calculate summary statistics we used ½ the LOD for samples below the laboratories limits of detection. See text for study area names.

Study Area	Year	N	Arithmetic				Geometric		
			Mean	Median	SD	SE	Mean	Upper 95% CI	Lower 95% CI
APIS	2006	8	125	112	95	33	98.8	165.1	59.1
	2007	6	52.8	50.0	28.5	11.6	46.1	73.4	29.0
	2008	5	58.0	65.5	29.3	13.1	51.4	84.7	31.2
LSSS	2007	6	88.9	89.4	34.7	14.2	81.9	119.8	56.0
	2008	4	36.6	40.1	11.3	5.6	35.0	49.7	24.6
U-SACN	2006	11	10.2	9.55	1.99	0.60	10.0	11.1	9.1
	2007	8	10.8	9.79	2.95	1.04	10.5	12.4	9.0
L-SACN	2006	3	156	118	95	55	139	268	72
	2007	4	68.8	67.0	25.1	12.6	65.2	94.7	44.9
	2008	7	85.0	92.9	30.4	11.5	79.4	108.2	58.3
	2009	9	90.8	73.4	35.2	11.7	85.5	108.0	67.6
MISS	2006	10	100	85.4	77.0	24.3	84.5	120.3	59.3
	2007	11	92.2	99.5	42.3	12.8	84.0	109.8	64.3
	2008	15	91.7	94.2	32.3	8.3	86.4	104.1	71.8
	2009	18	68.8	73.0	25.3	6.0	63.1	78.2	50.9
Pools 3+4	2008	15	112	109	27	7	109	124	96
	2009	12	104	103	18	5	103	113	93

Table 9. Geometric mean concentrations (*ug*/L) of 15 PCB congeners in plasma of bald eagle nestlings from six study areas, 2006-2009. Geometric means are estimates from mixed effects models.

Congener	APIS	LSSS	Pools 3&4	MISS	L-SACN	U-SACN
077/110	0.6	1.2	5.4	3.2	4.5	0.1
099	0.9	0.8	2.9	1.7	2.4	0.1
118	2.8	2.4	5.1	3.2	4.8	0.2
123/149	0.5	1.0	3.0	1.8	2.3	0.1
128	1.3	1.1	2.0	1.1	1.7	0.1
132/153/105	8.2	7.1	10.9	6.8	9.0	0.5
146	1.7	1.5	1.8	1.2	1.5	0.1
163/138	9.2	8.3	12.7	7.9	10.8	0.6
170/190	2.3	1.9	1.8	1.4	1.5	0.1
180	6.2	5.3	4.7	3.6	3.9	0.4
183	1.4	1.2	1.3	0.9	1.0	0.1
187/182	2.5	2.3	1.7	1.4	1.4	0.2
194	1.4	1.1	1.0	0.8	0.7	0.1
201	2.5	2.2	1.6	1.3	1.2	0.1
203/196	3.0	2.6	2.0	1.6	1.5	0.1

Table 10. Results of mixed effects models comparing levels of 15 PCB congeners in bald eagle plasma among six study areas listed from the highest geometric mean levels on the left to the lowest on the right. Those separated by "~" do not differ significantly; those separated by ">" do. A study area listed in parentheses is intermediate (i.e., among groups that otherwise differ significantly).

Congener(s)	P-value	Study area differences
077/110	<0.001	Pools 3&4 ~ (L-SACN) > MISS > LSSS ~ APIS > U-SACN
099	<0.001	Pools 3&4 ~ (L-SACN) > MISS > APIS ~ LSSS > U-SACN
118	<0.001	Pools 3&4 ~ (L-SACN ~ MISS ~ APIS) > LSSS > U-SACN
123/149	<0.001	Pools 3&4 ~ (L-SACN) > MISS > LSSS ~ APIS > U-SACN
128	<0.001	Pools 3&4 ~ (L-SACN ~ APIS ~ LSSS) > MISS > U-SACN
132/153/105	<0.001	Pools 3&4 ~ (L-SACN ~ APIS ~ LSSS) > MISS > U-SACN
146	<0.001	Pools 3&4 ~ (APIS ~ L-SACN ~ LSSS) > MISS > U-SACN
163/138	<0.001	Pools 3&4 ~ (L-SACN ~ APIS ~ LSSS) > MISS > U-SACN
170/190	<0.001	APIS ~ LSSS ~ Pools 3&4 ~ L-SACN ~ MISS > U-SACN
180	<0.001	APIS ~ (LSSS ~ Pools 3&4 ~ L-SACN) > MISS > U-SACN
183	<0.001	APIS ~ Pools 3&4 ~ LSSS ~ L-SACN ~ MISS > U-SACN
187/182	<0.001	APIS ~ LSSS ~ (Pools 3&4) > MISS ~ L-SACN > U-SACN
194	<0.001	APIS ~ (LSSS ~ Pools 3&4) > MISS ~ L-SACN > U-SACN
201	<0.001	APIS ~ (LSSS ~ Pools 3&4 ~ MISS) > L-SACN > U-SACN
203/196	<0.001	APIS ~ (LSSS ~ Pools 3&4) > MISS ~ L-SACN > U-SACN
Total PCBs	<0.001	Pools 3&4 ~ (L-SACN ~ MISS) > APIS ~ LSSS > U-SACN

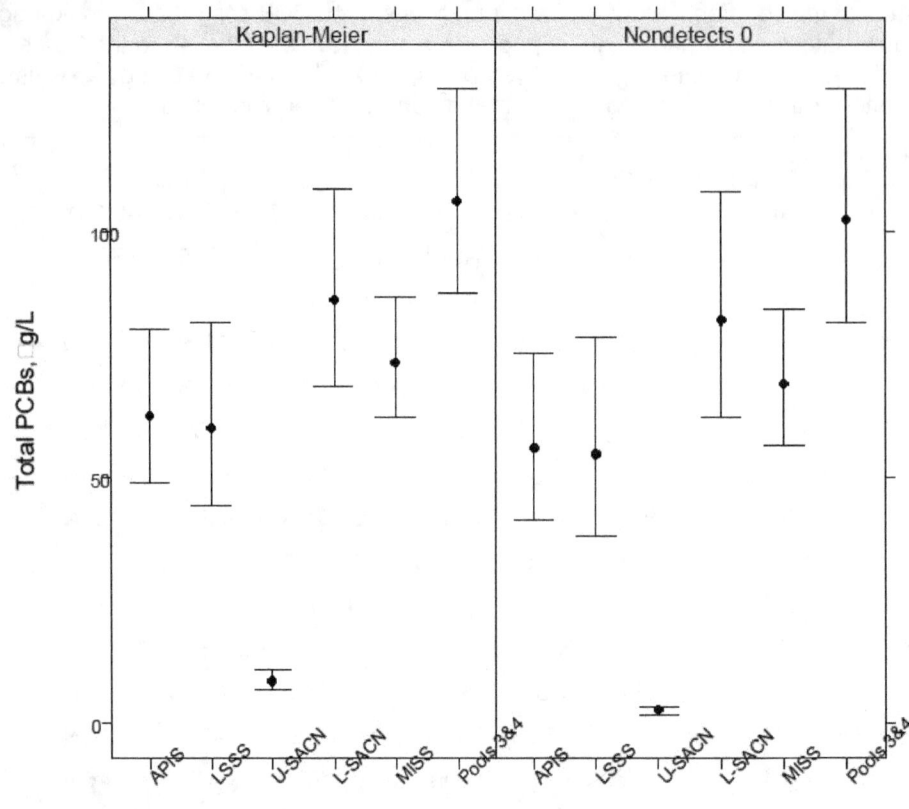

Figure 11. Estimated geometric mean concentrations and 95% confidence intervals for total PCB in bald eagle nestlings sampled in six study areas in the upper Midwest, 2006-2009. The left panel shows total PCB as calculated by the Kaplan-Meier nonparametric procedure; the right panel shows total PCB as calculated by replacing congener concentrations below the limit of detection by zeroes.

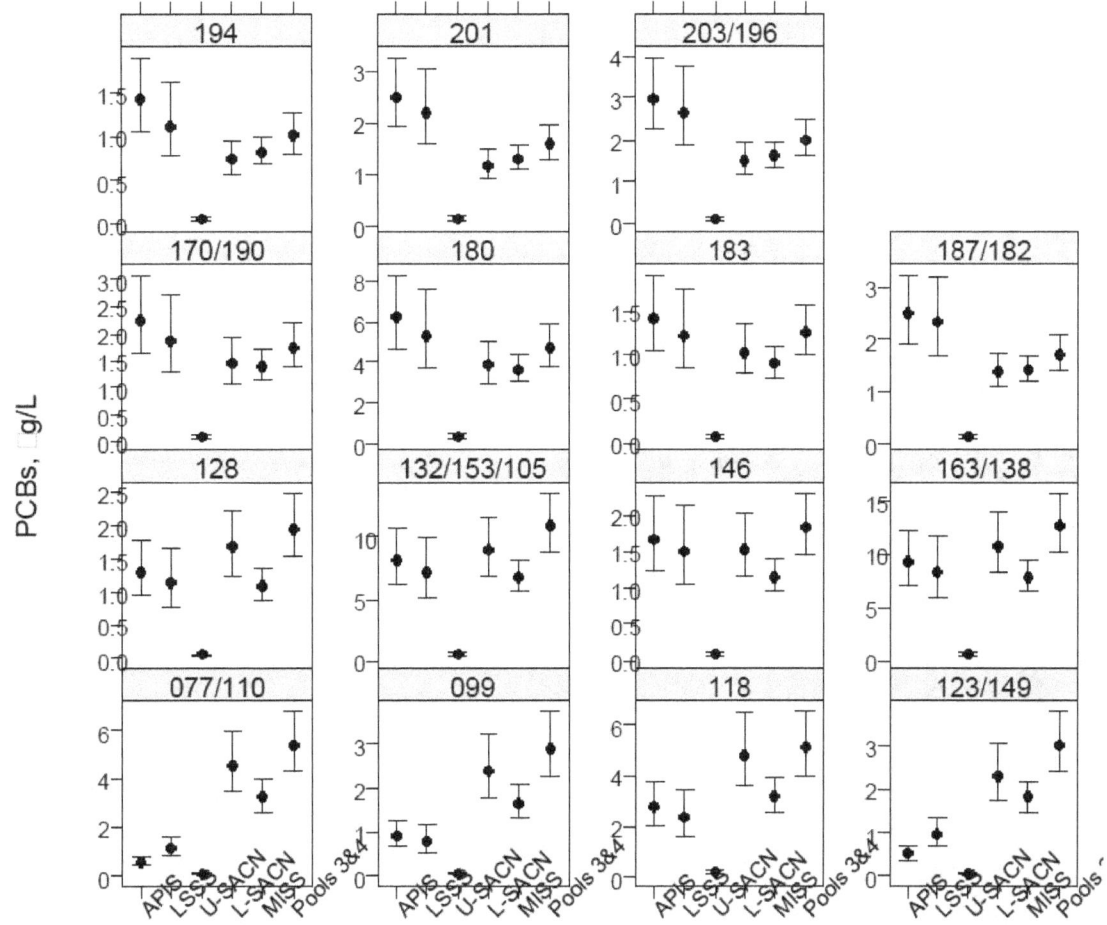

PCBs, g/L

Study area

Figure 12. Estimated geometric mean concentrations and 95% confidence intervals for 15 PCB congeners in bald eagle nestlings sampled in six study areas, 2006-2009. Geometric means and confidence intervals were estimated from mixed effects models.

Emerging Contaminants of Concern

PBDEs

We detected PBDEs in all bald eagle nestlings sampled, with geometric mean levels ranging from 1.39 *ug*/L at U-SACN to 16.8 *ug*/L at MISS (Table 11). Levels were particularly high in nestlings from Pig's Eye Lake in South St. Paul, Minnesota, (MISS) and from one nestling sampled in 2007 in the LSSS study area (Figure 13). Otherwise, total PBDE concentrations were uniformly ≤15 *ug*/L on U-SACN and ≤30 *ug*/L elsewhere.

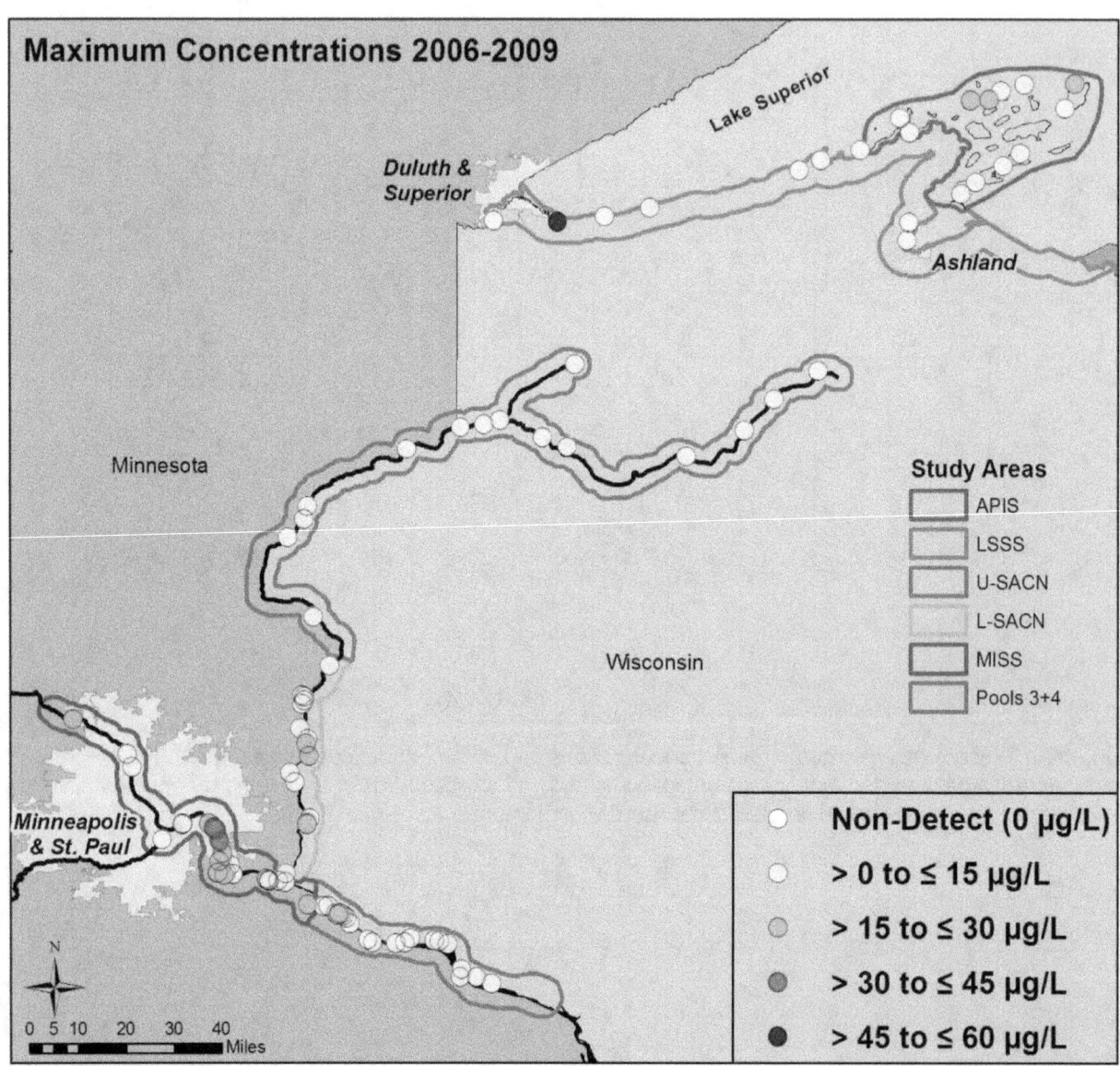

Figure 13. Maximum concentrations of total PBDE in plasma of bald eagle nestlings from all nests sampled across six study areas, 2006-2009.

Table 11. Sample size, measures of central tendency, and variability of total PBDE (*ug*/L) in plasma from bald eagle nestlings, 2006-2009. To calculate summary statistics we used ½ the LOD for samples below the laboratories detection limits. See text for study area names.

| Study Area | Year | N | Arithmetic | | | | Geometric | | |
			Mean	Median	SD	SE	Mean	Upper 95% CI	Lower 95% CI
APIS	2006	8	16.5	12.5	9.2	3.3	14.1	22.0	9.0
	2007	6	8.94	8.44	3.52	1.44	8.39	11.47	6.14
	2008	5	6.91	7.54	1.45	0.65	6.78	8.24	5.58
LSSS	2007	6	18.0	14.2	13.6	5.6	15.1	24.5	9.4
	2008	4	6.47	6.18	2.32	1.16	6.17	8.78	4.33
U-SACN	2006	11	1.42	1.29	0.29	0.09	1.39	1.57	1.23
	2007	8	1.69	1.22	1.09	0.39	1.49	2.08	1.07
L-SACN	2006	3	14.1	12.8	7.7	4.4	12.6	24.2	6.6
	2007	4	6.53	6.29	2.76	1.38	6.09	9.40	3.94
	2008	7	6.13	6.81	2.16	0.82	5.76	7.72	4.30
	2009	9	12.4	9.68	5.17	1.72	11.6	15.0	8.9
MISS	2006	10	16.0	13.5	7.2	2.3	14.7	19.3	11.1
	2007	11	18.7	13.3	10.1	3.0	16.8	22.1	12.7
	2008	15	14.4	14.7	4.1	1.1	13.8	16.3	11.8
	2009	18	13.6	12.1	6.1	1.4	12.5	15.1	10.3
Pools 3+4	2008	15	9.74	9.57	3.24	0.84	9.27	10.92	7.86
	2009	12	10.4	10.3	2.7	0.8	10.1	11.6	8.9

Five of the nine PBDE congeners we measured were detected in $\geq 80\%$ of samples and could be tested for significance among areas. All five of these congeners had significantly lower concentrations in eaglets from the upper St. Croix River, slightly higher concentrations in eaglets from the lower St. Croix, and often the highest concentrations in eaglets from the Mississippi River and Lake Superior regions (Figure 14, Tables 12 and 13).

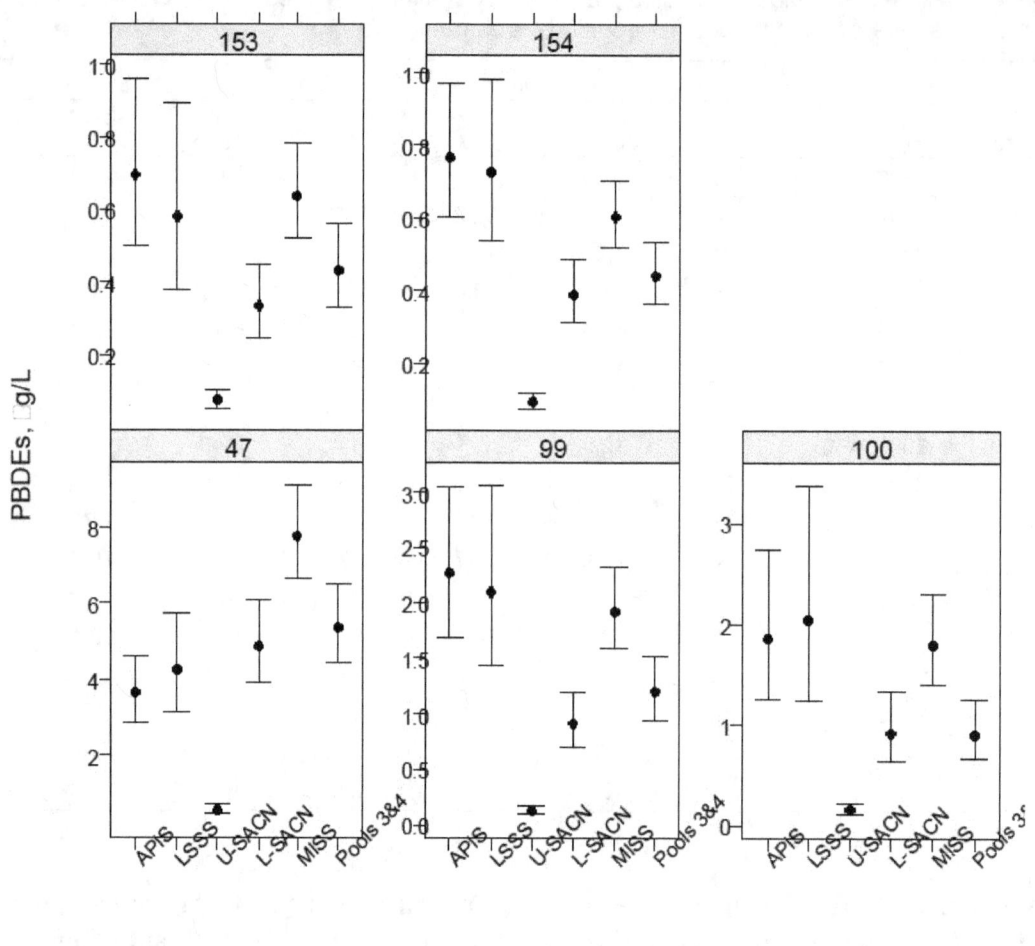

Figure 14. Estimated geometric means and 95% confidence intervals of five PBDE congeners in plasma from bald eagle nestlings sampled in six study areas, 2006-2009.

Table 12. Results of mixed effects models comparing concentrations of five PBDE congeners found in bald eagle plasma in six study areas. Study areas are listed from the highest geometric mean concentration on the left to the lowest on the right. Those separated by "~" do not differ significantly; those separated by a greater than sign ">" do. Study areas in parentheses are intermediate from the next lowest region (i.e., intermediate between two groups that otherwise differ significantly).

Congener	P-value	Study area differences
47	<0.001	MISS > Pools 3&4 ~ L-SACN ~ LSSS ~ APIS > U-SACN
99	<0.001	APIS ~ LSSS ~ MISS > Pools 3&4 ~ L-SACN > U-SACN
100	<0.001	LSSS ~ APIS ~ MISS > Pools 3&4 ~ L-SACN > U-SACN
153	<0.001	APIS ~ MISS ~ (LSSS ~ Pools 3&4) > L-SACN > U-SACN
154	<0.001	APIS ~ LSSS ~ (MISS) > Pools 3&4 ~ L-SACN > U-SACN

Table 13. Geometric mean concentrations (*ug*/L) of five PBDE congeners in bald eagle plasma from six study areas. Geometric means are estimates from mixed effects models. One-half the LOD was substituted for the concentration when observations were below the limits of detection.

Congener	APIS	LSSS	U-SACN	L-SACN	MISS	Pools 3&4
47	3.6	4.3	0.6	4.9	7.8	5.4
99	2.3	2.1	0.1	0.9	1.9	1.2
100	1.9	2.0	0.2	0.9	1.8	0.9
153	0.7	0.6	0.1	0.3	0.6	0.4
154	0.8	0.7	0.1	0.4	0.6	0.4

PFCs

In 2006 and 2007 we measured only two PFC analytes, PFOA and PFOS, whereas in 2008 and 2009 we measured 14 additional analytes for a total of 16 (Appendix A). Considering just PFOA and PFOS for all four years, PFOS accounted for the majority of the PFC volume with geometric means ranging from 13.4 *ug*/L at U-SACN in 2007 to 1580 *ug*/L at L-SACN in 2006 (upper portion of Table 14). Concentrations of PFOA were much lower, with geometric means ranging from 0.122 *ug*/L at L-SACN in 2009 to 4.97 *ug*/L at APIS in 2008 (lower portion of Table 14).

In 2008 and 2009, when all 16 analytes were measured, we found total PFC concentrations to be highest in a stretch of the Mississippi River below St. Paul, Minnesota, and at a few nests on L-SACN (Figure 15). The lowest levels were found in Lake Superior study areas (U-SACN was not sampled in 2008 and 2009). This pattern was also evident for PFOS, the congener that contributes more than 50% of the total PFC load by volume. PFOS made up a greater proportion of total PFCs in eaglets from the Mississippi River study areas (68%) compared to those from the Lake Superior study areas (53%; Figure 16).

Differences in the proportions of PFDS, PFuDA, and PFNA in the Mississippi River versus the Lake Superior nestlings were also clearly evident (Figure 16). PFDS composed 26% of the Mississippi River PFC volume but only 1% at Lake Superior. By contrast PFuDA and PFNA both made up a greater proportion of PFCs in the Lake Superior nestlings (16% and 15% at Lake

Superior versus 1% each on the Mississippi River respectively). Overall, PFC analytes were more evenly proportioned in Lake Superior eaglets than those on the Mississippi River.

Ten of the 16 PFC analytes passed our quality control criteria and could be tested for differences among study areas with mixed effects models. Six of these analytes were affected by either weight or age of the eaglet sampled (Table 15). The age and weight of eaglets sampled were highly correlated (r = 0.79; P <0.001; Pearson correlation coefficient). Because of this strong correlation, if the concentration of an analyte increases with one of these factors, it is likely to increase with the other. We used the Akaike Information Criterion (AIC; Burnham and Anderson 1998) to select the best fitting model for each analyte among three models, including (1) study area alone, (2) study area and age, and (3) study area and weight. Five PFC analytes (PFHxS, PFNA, PFTeDA, PFTrDA, and PFuDA) increased significantly with the weight of the eaglet, while one analyte, PFOS, increased significantly with the age of the eaglet. Four analytes, PFDA, PFDS, PFHpS, and PFOA, were not significantly related to either weight or age. For analytes that increased most significantly with weight, the rate of increase on the log scale ranged from 0.09 to 0.13 per kg (Table 15). These correspond to increases of 23% to 35% in analyte concentration per kilogram of body weight. The log of PFOS concentration increased at a rate of 0.013 per day, corresponding to an increase in concentration of 3% per day. To account for these relationships, we included age and weight as covariates in the mixed effects models for the following comparisons among study areas.

When comparing study areas three distinct patterns emerged: (1) U-SACN consistently had the lowest concentrations of all PFC analytes; (2) APIS and LSSS had the highest concentrations of PFNA, PFTrDA, PFOA, and PFuDA; and (3) MISS and Pools 3&4 had the highest concentrations of PFDS, PFOS, PFHpS, and PFHxS (Figure 17, Tables 16 and 17). The lower SACN study area alternated between the latter two patterns, but more often followed the Mississippi River study areas. The striking difference in spatial distribution in the levels of some analytes in Lake Superior eaglets compared to those in the Mississippi River is illustrated by PFOS, PFOA, and PFDS (Figures 18, 19, and 20, respectively).

Table 14. Sample size, measures of central tendency, and variability of total PFOS (upper table) and PFOA (lower) (ug/L) in plasma from bald eagle nestlings, 2006-2009. To calculate summary statistics we used ½ the LOD for samples below the laboratories limits of detection. See text for study area names.

| Study Area | Year | N | Arithmetic | | | | Geometric | | |
			Mean	Median	SD	SE	Mean	Upper 95% CI	Lower 95% CI
PFOS:									
APIS	2006	8	187	195	75	26	174	230	131
	2007	6	164	130	103	42	146	215	99
	2008	5	172	150	49	22	167	211	132
LSSS	2007	6	191	175	77	31	177	252	124
	2008	4	153	155	28	14	151	181	126
U-SACN	2006	11	30.5	29.0	19.4	5.9	26.3	36.7	18.8
	2007	8	14.5	13.5	6.2	2.2	13.4	17.8	10.1
L-SACN	2006	3	1810	2300	942	544	1580	3432	731
	2007	4	345	350	270	135	169	1100	26
	2008	7	539	460	248	94	496	682	361
	2009	9	466	530	156	52	439	561	344
MISS	2006	10	1360	1250	640	202	1250	1630	954
	2007	11	828	830	250	75	791	958	653
	2008	15	846	860	339	88	749	1021	550
	2009	18	665	645	368	87	541	762	385
Pools 3+4	2008	15	942	900	318	82	890	1065	744
	2009	12	746	800	217	63	717	848	606
PFOA:									
APIS	2006	8	2.53	2.40	1.46	0.52	2.13	3.34	1.35
	2007	6	5.80	2.90	5.66	2.31	3.76	8.61	1.64
	2008	5	6.28	4.30	4.37	1.95	4.97	10.09	2.45
LSSS	2007	6	1.32	1.05	0.68	0.28	1.19	1.75	0.81
	2008	4	2.59	2.10	1.95	0.97	2.07	4.45	0.97
U-SACN	2006	11	0.285	0.330	0.154	0.047	0.222	0.369	0.134
	2007	8	0.726	0.720	0.045	0.016	0.725	0.756	0.695
L-SACN	2006	3	0.430	0.330	0.255	0.147	0.385	0.730	0.203
	2007	4	3.10	0.835	4.602	2.301	1.50	5.19	0.43
	2008	7	0.304	0.270	0.117	0.044	0.285	0.383	0.212
	2009	9	0.159	0.140	0.127	0.042	0.122	0.201	0.075
MISS	2006	10	1.13	0.625	1.138	0.360	0.818	1.312	0.509
	2007	11	1.26	1.20	0.35	0.11	1.22	1.43	1.05
	2008	15	0.695	0.580	0.316	0.082	0.639	0.789	0.518
	2009	18	0.564	0.425	0.423	0.100	0.416	0.620	0.279
Pools 3+4	2008	15	0.676	0.760	0.297	0.077	0.600	0.791	0.455
	2009	12	0.383	0.265	0.281	0.081	0.309	0.450	0.212

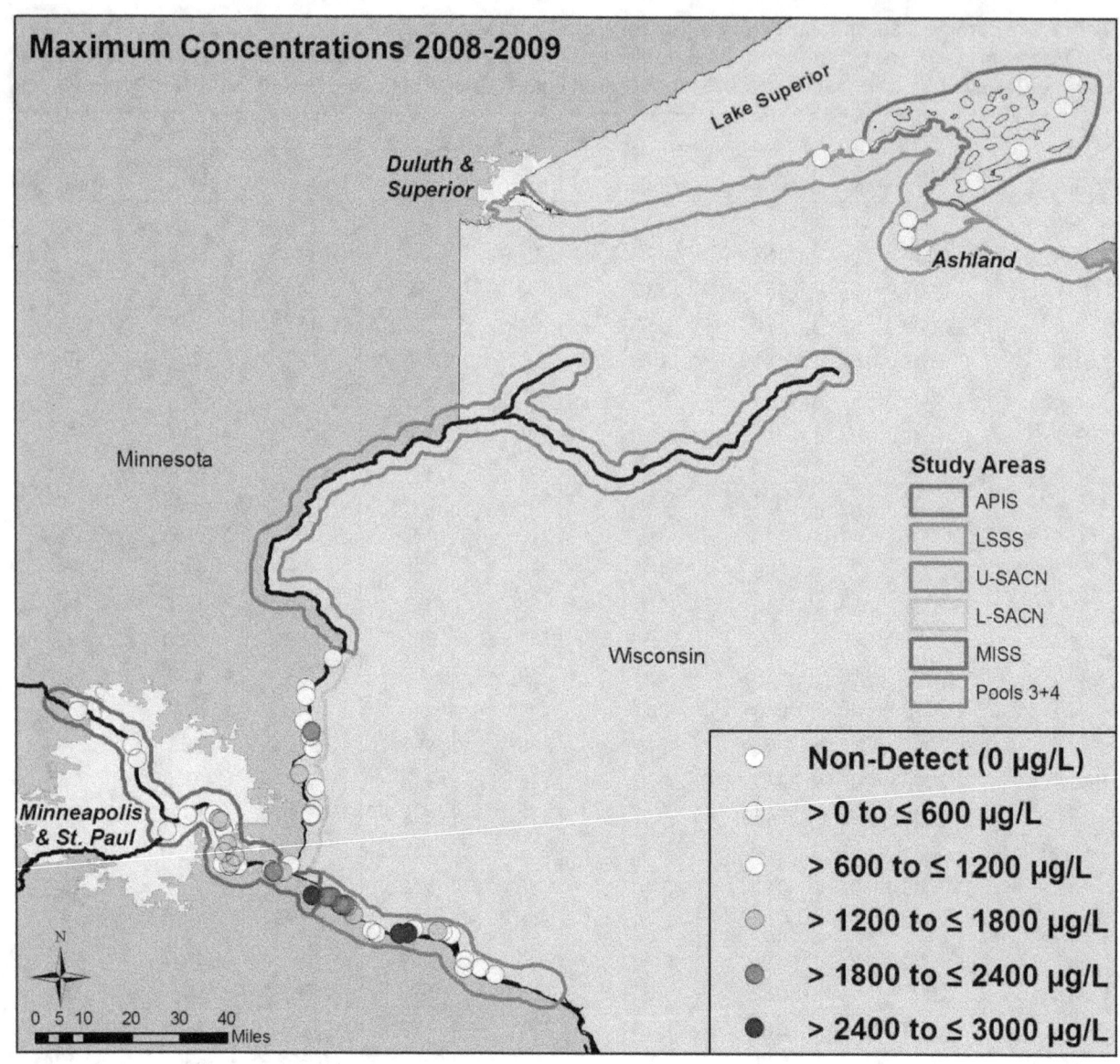

Figure 15. Maximum concentrations of total PFC in plasma of bald eagle nestlings from all nests sampled across six study areas, 2008 and 2009.

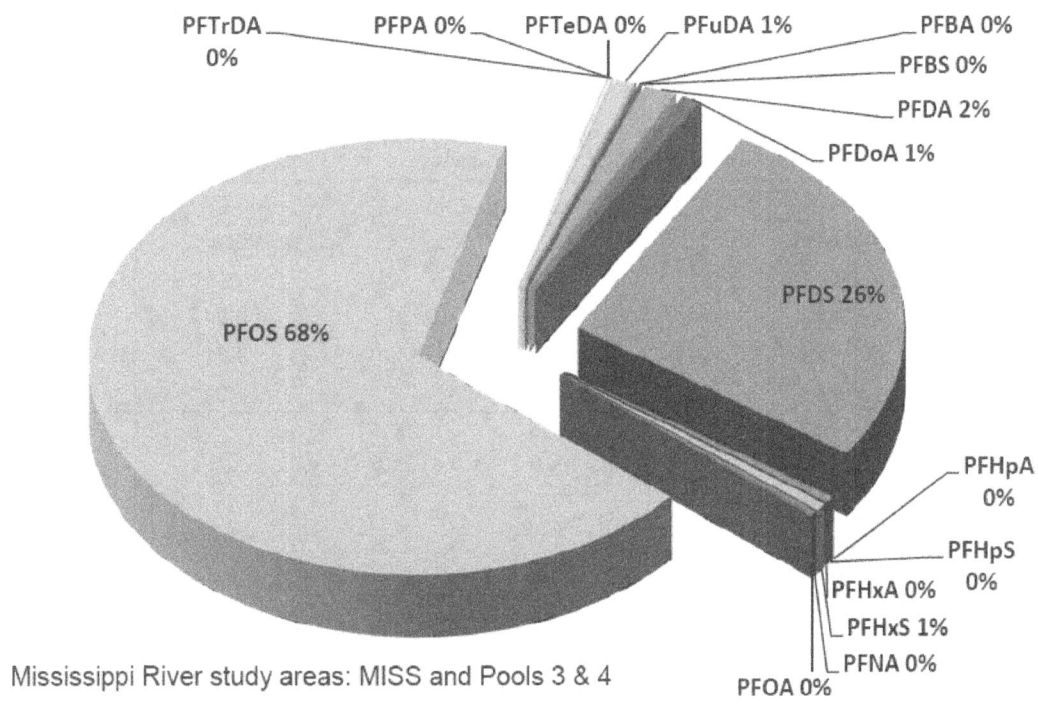

Mississippi River study areas: MISS and Pools 3 & 4

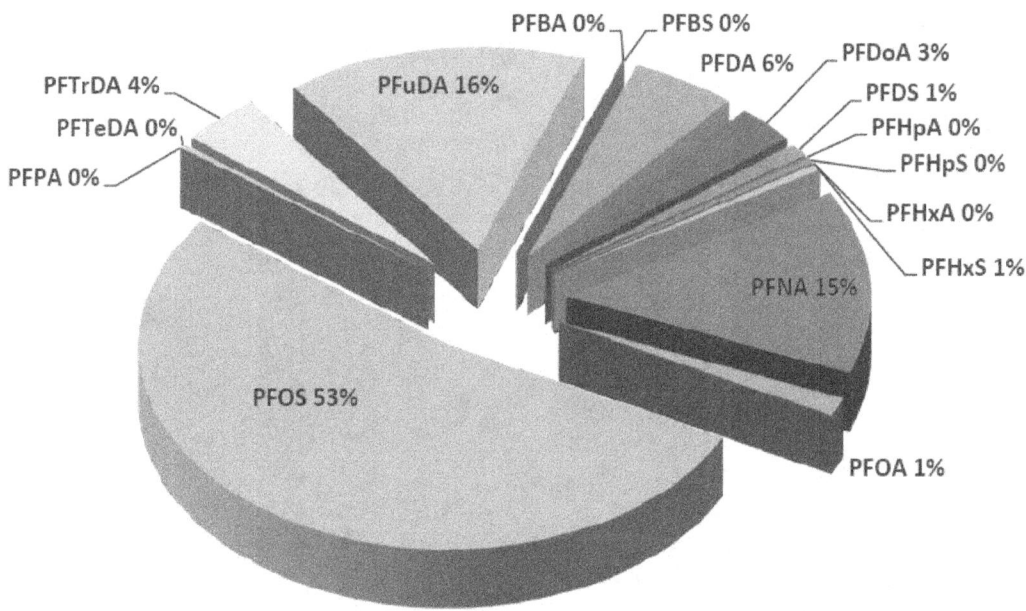

Lake Superior study areas: APIS and LSSS

Figure 16. Percent by volume of different PFC congeners in bald eagle plasma, 2008 and 2009; top chart shows the Mississippi River study areas (MISS and Pools 3&4) and the bottom chart shows the Lake Superior study areas (APIS and LSSS).

Table 15. Relation of age and weight of nestling bald eagles on the levels of six PFC analytes (*u*g/L). These covariates were included in mixed effects models when examining differences in PFC concentrations among study areas. Four other PFC analytes showed no relation to age or weight (P >0.05).

Congener	Covariate	Estimate (SE)	P-value
PFHxS	Weight	0.13 (0.056)	0.03
PFNA	weight	0.11 (0.028)	<0.001
PFOS	Age	0.013 (0.0024)	<0.001
PFTeDA	Weight	0.13 (0.045)	0.01
PFTrDA	Weight	0.09 (0.034)	0.01
PFuDA	Weight	0.11 (0.044)	0.01

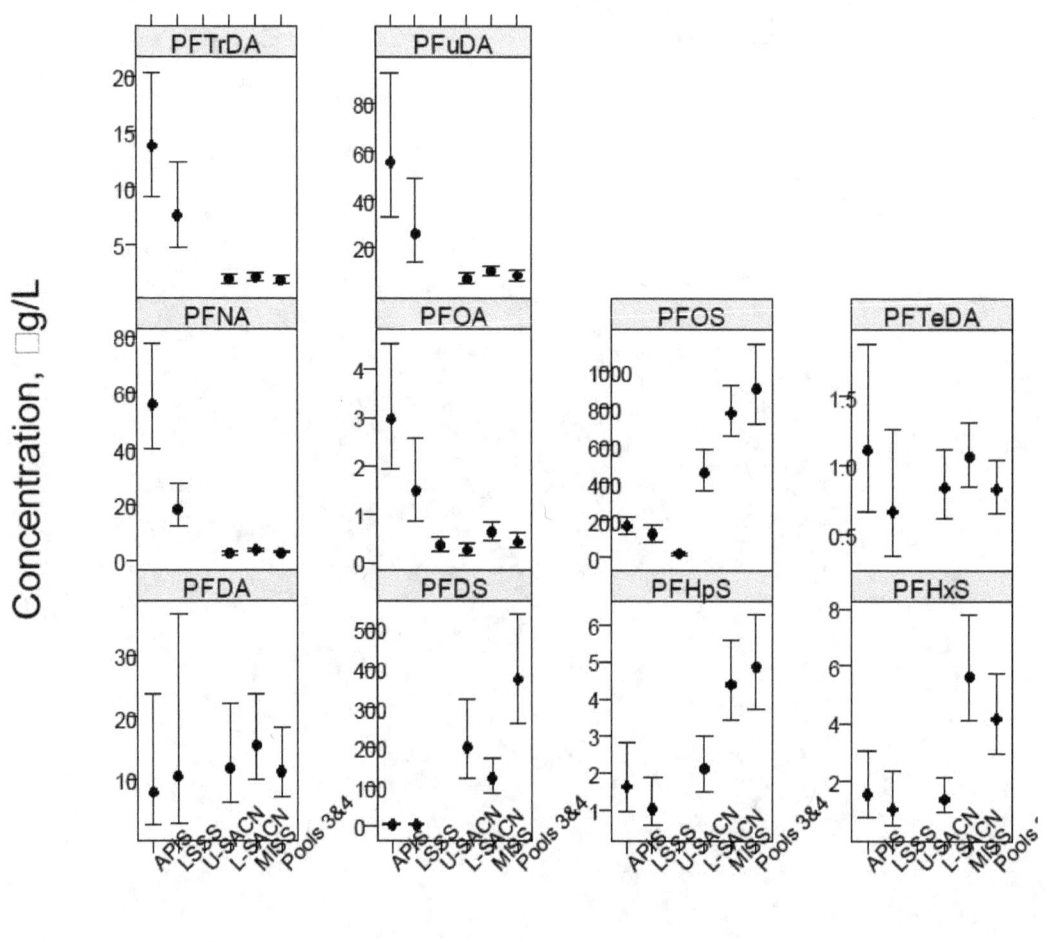

Figure 17. Estimated geometric mean concentrations and 95% confidence intervals of 10 PFC congeners in bald eagle nestlings sampled in six study areas in the upper Midwest, 2006-2009.

40

Table 16. Results of mixed effects models comparing concentrations of six PFC congeners found in bald eagle plasma at six study areas. Areas are listed from highest geometric mean concentration on the left to the lowest on the right. Those separated by "~" do not differ significantly; those separated by a greater than sign ">" do. A study area in parentheses is intermediate from the next lowest study area (i.e., intermediate between two groups that otherwise differ significantly).

Congener	*P*-value	Study area differences
PFDA	0.74	none
PFDS	< 0.001	Pools 3&4 ~ L-SACN ~ MISS > LSSS ~ APIS
PFHpS	< 0.001	Pools 3&4 ~ MISS > L-SACN ~ APIS ~ LSSS
PFHxS	<0.001	MISS ~ (Pools 3&4 ~ APIS) > L-SACN ~ LSSS
PFNA	<0.001	APIS > LSSS > MISS > Pools 3&4 ~ L-SACN
PFOA	< 0.001	APIS ~ LSSS > MISS ~ Pools 3&4 ~ U-SACN ~ L-SACN
PFOS	<0.001	Pools 3&4 ~ MISS > L-SACN > APIS ~ LSSS > U-SACN
PFTeDA	0.39	none
PFTrDA	<0.001	APIS ~ LSSS > MISS ~ L-SACN ~ Pools 3&4
PFuDA	<0.001	APIS ~ (LSSS ~ MISS) > Pools 3&4 ~ L-SACN

Table 17. Geometric mean concentrations (*u*g/L) of 10 PFC congeners in bald eagle plasma from six study areas. Geometric means are estimates from mixed effects models. One-half the LOD was substituted for the concentration when observations were below the laboratories limits of detection.

Congener	APIS	LSSS	Pools 3&4	MISS	L-SACN	U-SACN
PFDA	7.9	10.6	11.3	15.5	11.9	.
PFDS	2.9	3.5	373	122	198	.
PFHpS	1.6	1.0	4.8	4.4	2.1	.
PFHxS	1.5	1.0	4.2	5.6	1.4	.
PFNA	55.8	18.2	2.8	3.8	2.7	.
PFOA	2.9	1.5	0.4	0.6	0.3	0.4
PFOS	164	121	905	776	456	17.2
PFTeDA	1.1	0.7	0.8	1.1	0.8	.
PFTrDA	13.7	7.6	1.9	2.2	1.9	.
PFuDA	55.4	26.0	8.2	10.2	7.0	.

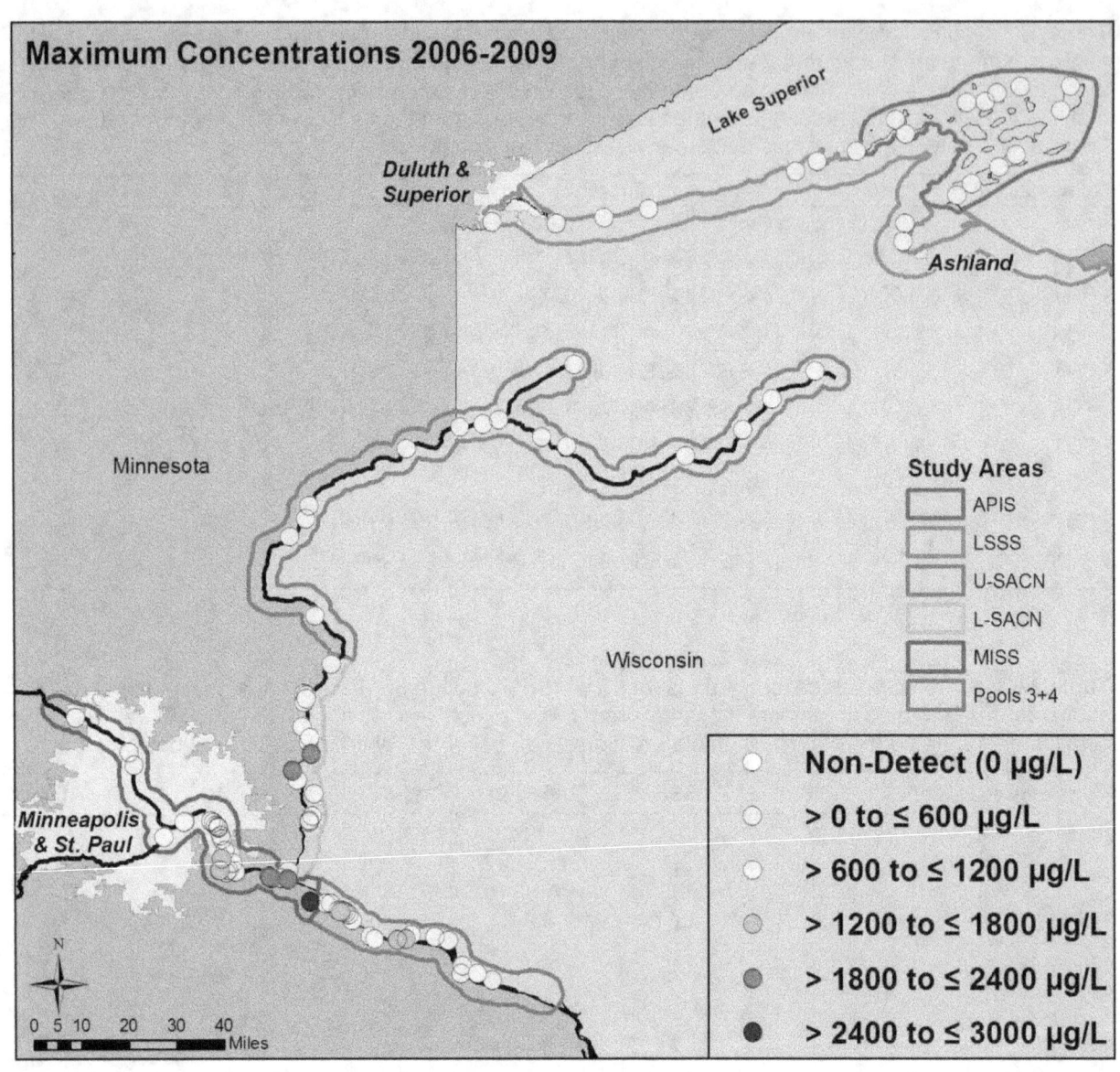

Figure 18. Maximum concentrations of PFOS found in plasma of bald eagle nestlings from all nests sampled across six study areas, 2006-2009.

42

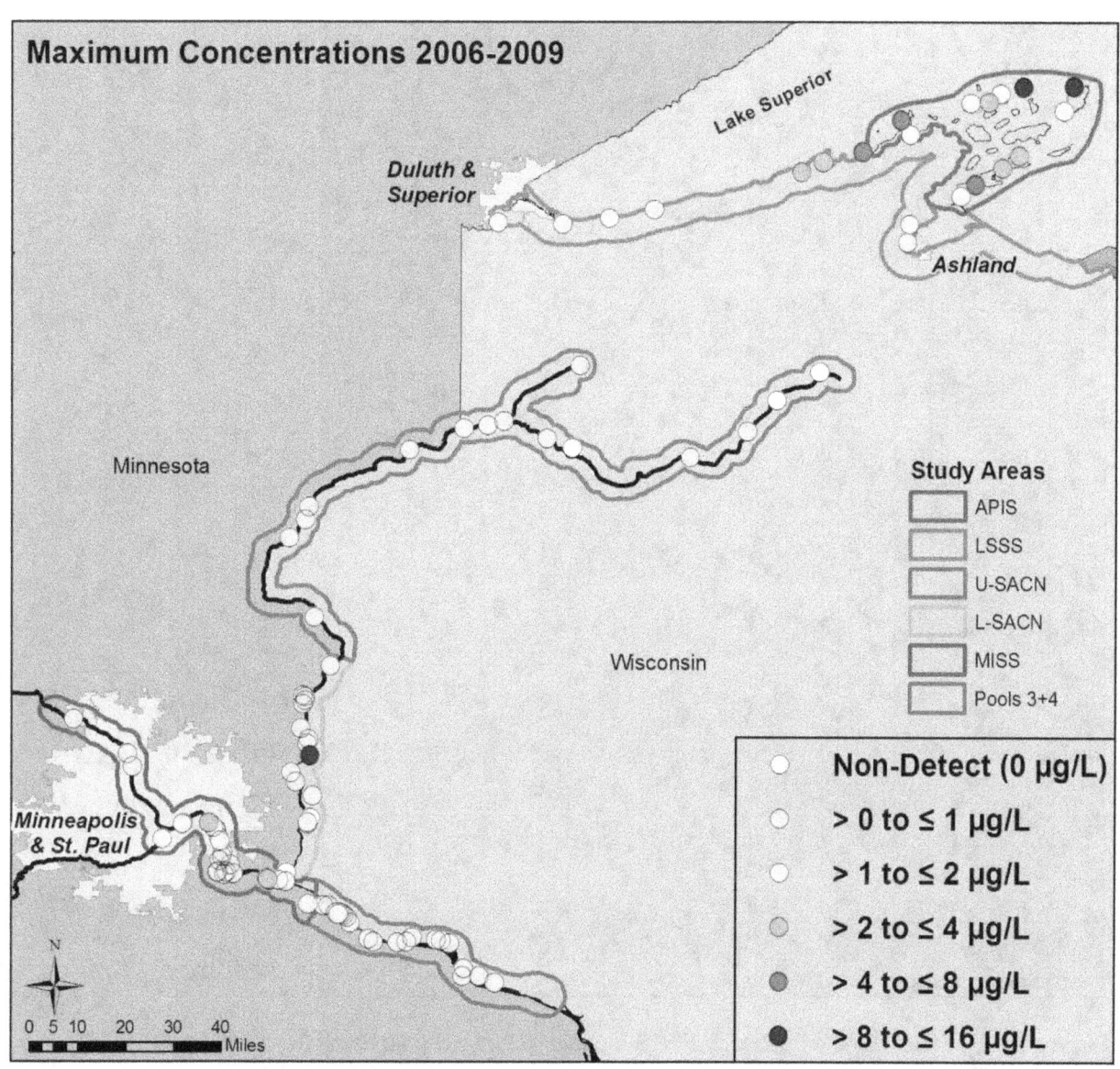

Figure 19. Maximum concentrations of PFOA found in plasma of bald eagle nestlings from all nests sampled across six study areas, 2006-2009.

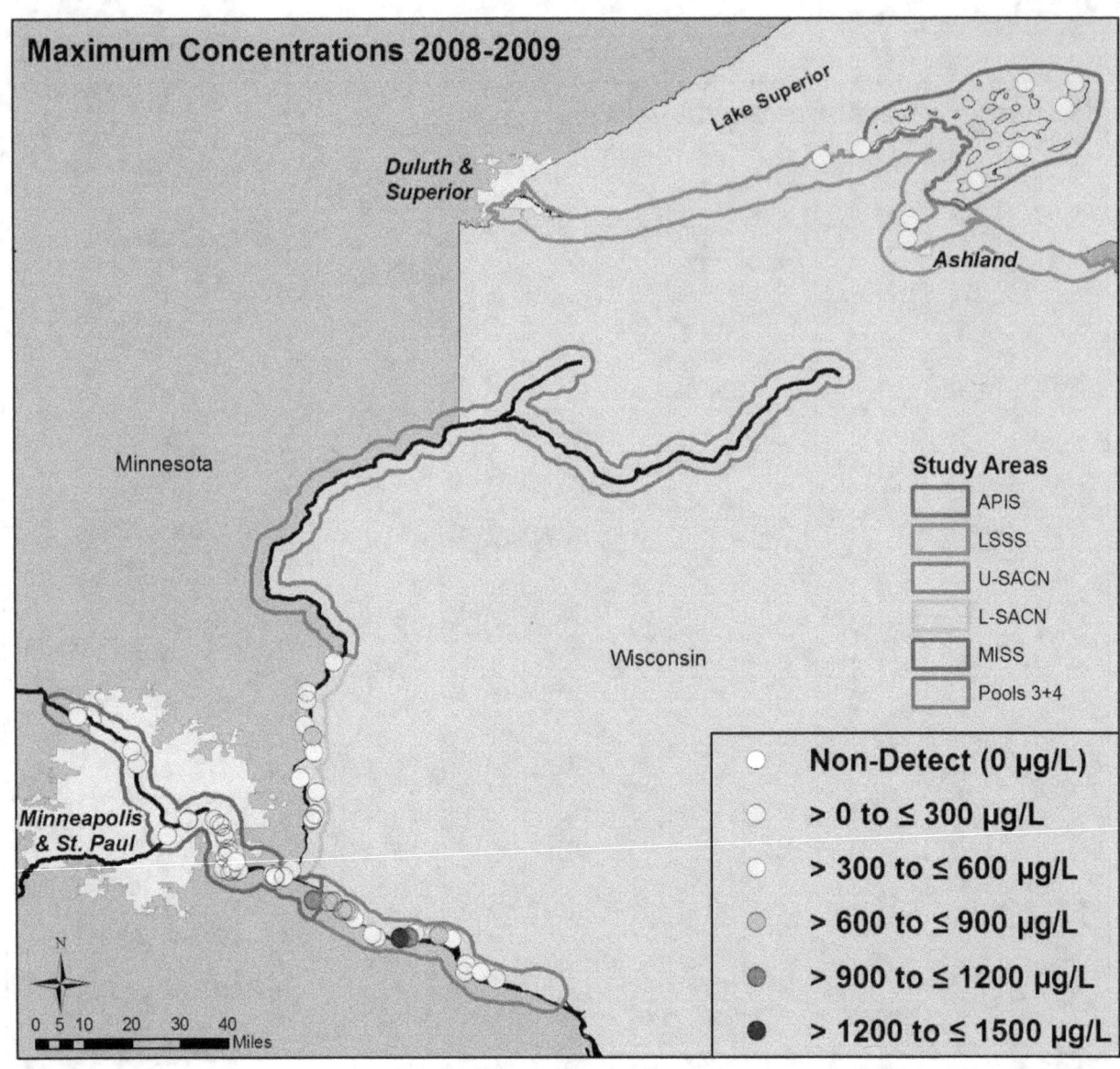

Figure 20. Maximum concentrations of PFDS found in plasma of bald eagle nestlings from all nests sampled across six study areas, 2008-2009. The U-SACN study area was not sampled in 2008 and 2009.

Discussion

Productivity and Mortality

On average the bald eagle population across the study region exceeded the thresholds of $\geq 50\%$ nest success and ≥ 1.0 young per active territory considered necessary for sustaining a healthy bald eagle population (Wiemeyer et al. 1984). In particular, bald eagles at MISS and L-SACN were highly productive. One nest at MISS (Pig's Eye Island number one) had four young in both 2006 and 2009 and three in 2007 and 2008. Nests with three young were common in the MISS study area, and we found eagles nesting within a kilometer of each other. Nest success and productivity at APIS and LSSS were lower, and in 2008 productivity measures for the APIS population were at the threshold for a healthy population. Nonetheless, the number and range of nesting bald eagles has been expanding across the region and we believe that the population is fundamentally healthy.

Bald eagles sampled in our study areas are part of a larger population, and their reproductive success and mortality rates are influenced by multiple factors. Dykstra et al. (2005) argued that productivity of bald eagles on Lake Superior, including both the APIS and LSSS study areas, was low at least partly because of low food availability - although other factors such as PCBs could not be ruled out. They measured prey delivery rates by adult bald eagles to nestlings and concluded that Lake Superior bald eagles made 56% fewer deliveries to the nest than breeding pairs in a comparable inland population (Dykstra 2005). Moreover, the authors calculated that the amount of energy received by Lake Superior nestlings in broods with two eaglets was less than typically expended for growth and development. Lake Superior is classified as an oligotrophic lake (i.e. unproductive) so it is reasonable to assume that foraging bald eagles need to work harder to attain food there than at more productive aquatic environments. The Lake Superior bald eagle population has recovered from lows of the 1960s, but at a much slower rate than inland populations. It is likely that nest success and productivity of eagles on Lake Superior will continue at lower levels relative to inland populations, and hence they will be more vulnerable to natural and human-caused perturbations like weather and contaminants.

We observed little direct mortality of young and could not determine the cause of four of the nine deaths that we documented. Of the non-study related mortalities, three were from natural causes and one died of disease. One nestling was euthanized after being found entangled in fishing line with a broken leg. We assume these estimates of mortality are low because we likely missed remains of nestlings removed by predators and scavengers.

Contaminant Levels and Spatial Patterns

Heavy Metals

Mercury

Nearly all of the mercury we measured in bald eagle feathers is assumed to be methylmercury, the most toxic form. Eagle nestlings get their mercury primarily from the fish they eat and nearly all (e.g., 99%; Grieb et al. 2009) of the mercury in fish is present as methylmercury. Eagle nestlings incorporate this mercury into their feathers while they grow (Lewis and Furness 1991) and the resulting levels serve as an indicator of methylmercury in their diet.

The geometric mean concentrations of mercury in feathers (2.69 to 6.08 ug/g wet wt.) were comparable or slightly lower than those measured elsewhere. Eagle nestlings in central Florida had feather concentrations of 3.23 ug/g wet wt., (1991-1993; Wood et al. 1996) and in South Carolina, concentrations of 3.06 ug/g dry weight (dry wt.; 1998-1999; Jagoe et al. 2002). Slightly higher concentrations were found in Maine, averaging 6.6 and 7.8 ug/g wet wt. (1991 and 1992) and these levels were not correlated with productivity rates, although any such relationship may have been masked by high concentrations of DDE (Welch 1994). Nearer to our study areas, Bowerman (1993) reported nestling feather mercury concentrations during 1985 to1989 of 8.8 ug/g wet wt. in the interior lower peninsula of Michigan, 8.1 ug/g in the interior upper peninsula, 8.0 ug/g at Lakes Michigan and Huron, 3.7 ug/g at Lake Erie, 8.7 ug/g at Lake Superior, and 20.2 ug/g at Voyageurs National Park in northern Minnesota. This study also reported a lack of relationship between mercury concentrations and productivity, but again, the analysis may have been confounded by high concentrations of organochlorines (Bowerman 1993).

Although mercury has been measured in adult and nestling feathers by several investigators, a threshold has not been determined for feathers of bald eagles. Eisler (1987) proposed that 5 ug/g in feathers might be cause for concern while others have suggested that >20 ug/g mercury in adult feathers should trigger an evaluation (Welsh 1994, Evers et al. 2004, DeSorbo and Evers 2007). We set a provisional threshold of 7.5 ug/g wet wt. in eaglet breast feathers, as proposed by Jagoe et al. (2002). During the four years of our study, this threshold was exceeded in two nestlings along the LSSS and in five nestlings from the U-SACN. In 2006 the geometric mean for the entire upper St. Croix study area exceeded this provisional level.

These attempts to set threshold values are based on effects at the population scale, but the levels at which sublethal effects occur are also important. Scheuhammer et al. (2008) showed that bald eagles could demethylate mercury in the brain but that significant neurochemical changes occurred with increasing levels of mercury in the brain. Effect levels were not reported by Scheuhammer et al. (2008), but we are currently collaborating with these investigators to correlate mercury levels in feathers to changes in brain chemistry in eagles.

We found mercury levels to be highest in eaglets from the upper St. Croix River and Lake Superior shoreline, and lowest in eaglets from the Apostle Islands and Mississippi River study areas. These patterns likely reflect water chemistry and drainage basin characteristics that influence the conversion of inorganic mercury (the dominant forms in atmospheric deposition) to methylmercury, the organic compound that bioaccumulates in organisms and biomagnifies in food webs. Many of the nestlings with high levels were from eagle territories immediately down river from extensive wetlands. For example, individual drainage basins for tributaries to the upper St. Croix River have ≥12% of their area classified as wetlands compared to <7% for the lower St. Croix, Mississippi River, and Apostle Islands. One nestling on the Lake Superior shoreline that was particularly high in mercury was from a nest at the mouth of the Amnicon River where wetlands comprise approximately 22% of the watershed (NLCD 2009).

The association between wetlands and methylmercury is well documented (Hurley et al. 1995, Wiener et al. 2003). Levels of both total mercury and methylmercury in water from eight streams in Wisconsin, Florida, and Oregon were highly correlated with the percent of wetlands within the drainages (Brigham et al. 2009). These same streams had top predatory fish with mercury levels that were positively correlated with the percent of wetlands in the drainage (Chasar et al. 2009). The streams studied by both Brigham et al. (2009) and Chasar et al. (2009) spanned large ranges in climate, landscape characteristics, atmospheric mercury deposition, and stream chemistry, but wetlands were a common factor in the availability and accumulation of mercury.

Similar findings were presented by Christensen et al. (2006) who examined the spatial variation of mercury in fish at 14 sites along the St. Croix River. They found that sites with mixed forest/wetland drainages had significantly higher median fish-tissue concentrations than sites with mixed forest/agricultural lands (i.e., few wetlands). Our findings at individual eagle nest sites correspond well with site-specific levels in fish found by Christensen et al. (2006).

In addition to wetlands there are other ecosystem parameters that contribute to mercury availability. Low alkalinity or low pH lakes, waters adjacent to uplands subjected to periodic flooding, and lakes and streams with high dissolved organic carbon (DOC) are all associated with high levels of mercury (numerous studies summarized in Wiener et al. 2003). All of these conditions can occur in the study areas we measured and they likely contribute to the overall mercury load in biota.

Recent data suggest a decline in the accumulation of mercury in sediments deposited in the region. Balogh et al. (2010) showed that mercury in upper Lake St. Croix, which serves as an indicator of deposits from the upper river, increased rapidly after 1900, leveled off in the 1960s, and declined through 2000. Using data from nearby Square Lake, these authors concluded that atmospheric inputs controlled mercury accumulation in upper Lake St. Croix sediments and that the recent (1990s) rates of mercury accumulation were 40% lower than the peak of the 1960s. Similarly, Evers (2005) showed that accumulation rates of mercury in lake sediments from coring studies in the northeastern U.S. peaked around 1980 with a subsequent decline. Both Evers (2005) and Balogh et al. (2010) attributed the declines in mercury accumulation rates to regulatory controls on emissions. Such controls began in the 1950s with local and state laws (e.g. California's Bay Area Air Pollution Control Law of 1955) and more broadly in 1965 with the passage of the National Emissions Standards Act in the United States. Nonetheless, the rate of mercury accumulation still greatly exceeds pre-industrial conditions.

In combination with a longer data set from the WDNR our data show that between 1991 and 2008 mercury levels declined at 3% per year in eaglet feathers from Lake Superior (Dykstra et al. 2010). Similar declines have been documented in other biota in the region. In inland northern Wisconsin lakes, mercury concentrations in blood of nestling common loons (*Gavia immer*) declined 4.9% annually from 1992 to 2000 (Fevold et al. 2003) and about 0.5% per year in walleye (*Sander vitreus*; 1982-2005; Rasmussen et al. 2007). By contrast, during this same time frame other studies showed no declines and even increases in mercury in some biota.

Mercury concentrations in eaglet plasma from inland lakes in Maine did not decrease between 1991 and 2006, nor did Hg concentrations in eagle eggs decline since the 1970s (DeSorbo and Evers 2007). In Minnesota lakes, mercury concentrations in predatory fish declined from 1982 through 1992 but then increased at 0.8% per year through 2006 (Monson 2009). In walleye from Wisconsin lakes there were mixed results in mercury trends depending on latitude: levels decreased 0.5% in northern lakes, increased 0.8% in southern lakes, and remained constant in middle latitudes over the period 1982-2005 (Rasmussen et al. 2007). For the Canadian portion of the Great Lakes, Bhavsar et al. (2010) reported that concentrations of mercury in walleye (fillet and whole fish) generally declined over three decades (mid 1970s-2007), but recent trends show a leveling off in Lake Ontario and possible increases in Lake Erie. In the Canadian Arctic, Braune et al. (2005) showed steady increases in total mercury in eggs of three species of sea birds from 1970 to 2005.

The methylation and accumulation of mercury in the food web is influenced by seasonal weather and climate patterns. Park et al. (2008) found that water temperature and the intensity of UV light were positively correlated with dissolved gaseous mercury in water. And Balogh et al. (2008) documented increases in methylmercury during major spring runoff events to streams in the Midwest. We found the highest levels of mercury in 2006 on the upper St Croix River, a year with an unusually warm and wet spring. For instance gridded 4 km isopleths of weather station data for the upper St. Croix area in 2006 shows 16-11 $^{\circ}$C (2-12 $^{\circ}$F) above 30-year normal temperatures in January, March, April, May and June with 20-80 mm above 30-year normal precipitation in March and April (PRISM 2010). We hypothesize that the high Hg levels in eaglets sampled in 2006 were the result of a warm, wet spring. The Wisconsin Initiative on Climate Change Impacts (WICCI), using global climate models for 1980-2055, projects a rise of 15-14 $^{\circ}$C (4.5 to 6 $^{\circ}$F) in spring temperatures and 2 to 2.5 cm above normal precipitation for the region immediately surrounding our study areas (WICCI 2010). If these climate forecasts are accurate, and mercury emissions are not reduced, then mercury levels may begin to increase in our study areas.

Lead

We found very little published information on levels of lead in breast feathers of bald eagle nestlings for comparison to our results. Lead is usually measured in blood and much research has been done to determine the lead-toxicity thresholds in blood of bald eagles. Lead levels are routinely measured in blood by veterinarians and raptor rehabilitators to determine if poisoning has occurred. However, blood levels may not be the most useful measure of lead exposure for long-term monitoring. Lead in blood will dissipate slowly over 30 to 40 days after exposure, whereas in feathers it will be integrated throughout the growth period (until molt). Feathers can also be sampled and analyzed in segments to establish exposure history (Finkelstein et al. 2010) and further compared with museum specimens for retrospective analyses (but see Pain et al. 2008 for cautions on this approach).

In our study the levels of lead in eaglet breast feathers ranged from .070 ug/g wet wt. (half the LOD) to 3.71 ug/g wet wt. Burger and Gochfeld (2009) reported a geometric mean of 0.769 ug/g dry wt. (n = two eaglet breast feathers) and 3.57 ug/g dry wt. (n = 17 adult breast feathers) from the Aleutian Islands, Alaska. Pain et al. (2008) found 1.05 to 14.3 ug/g dry wt. of lead in feathers of adult Spanish imperial eagles (*Aquila adalberti*), which feed primarily on fish and waterfowl, much like bald eagles in North America. The authors believed that the higher levels resulted from atmospheric deposition on the museum specimens following death of the birds. Martinez-Lopez et al. (2004) found 0.35 to 1.66 µg/g dry wt. of lead in feathers of three adult raptor species, including the booted eagle (*Hieraaetus pennatus*), that were from regions of Spain that were far from sources of metal contamination. Custer et al. (2008) reported <0.9 ug/g dry wt. of lead in feathers of nestling black-crowned night heron (*Nycticorax nycticorax*) in rural

Minnesota and 0.11-0.41 dry wt. at industrial sites in Delaware and Maryland. Lead poisoning has been of concern for the endangered California condor (*Gymnogyps californianus*). Two events of acute lead poisoning were recently documented in which concentrations of lead in feathers increased from pre-exposure levels of <0.3 *ug/g* dry wt. to just over 3.0 and 4.0 *ug/g* dry wt. with peak levels occurring within 20 days of the bird ingesting lead fragments from a hunter-killed pig (Finkelstein et al. 2010). Both of these birds were treated and survived, but a third condor died of lead poisoning with a peak of 55 *ug/g* of lead in feathers (Finkelstein et al. 2010). The lead levels in our eaglets were considerably less that the pre-exposure levels of these condors; however, differences between the species and their relative ages regarding uptake and shedding of lead into feathers is not well understood.

Lead poisoning in adult bald eagles has long been associated with their feeding on dead or crippled waterfowl contaminated with lead shot (Hennes 1985), however, retrospective and current studies suggest that many poisonings result from ingestion of hunter-crippled or killed terrestrial game (Kramer and Redig 1997, Martin et al. 2007, Pain et al. 2008, Redig et al. 2009, Lambertucci et al. 2010). Evidence from studies on common loons (Scheuhammer and Norris 1996) suggests that lead sinkers or fishing lures in fish eaten by eagles could also cause poisoning. In our case, hunter-killed game is not available to eaglets because most hunting occurs in fall. Fishing is common across the study areas, but if fishing lures and sinkers were the cause of the levels we observed, we would expect exposure to be distributed somewhat evenly across the six study areas. More likely, the hotspot at Pig's Eye Lake is related to the historical and current use of this area for waste disposal and wastewater treatment, the latter including urban run-off . The City of St. Paul used a 300-acre area up-gradient from Pig's Eye Lake as a dump from the mid-1950s to 1972 and the area is listed on the Minnesota Pollution Control Agency's (MPCA) Superfund list. From 1977 to 1985 the Metropolitan Waste Control Commission was permitted to dispose of ash from burned sewage sludge at this site. Currently, the city of St. Paul operates a wastewater treatment facility near the lake and effluent is discharged into the Mississippi River nearby. The relative contribution of these industrial/public sources to the lead we found in bald eagle nestlings is not known. The concentrations of lead in virtually all environmental media have declined significantly since the phase out of alkyl lead as an additive in gasoline (e.g., Wiener and Sandheinrich 2010). In the Upper Mississippi River, the annual accumulation of lead in sediments of Lake Pepin (Pool 4) in the 1990s was half of that in the 1960s (17 versus 35 tons, respectively)—the decade of peak lead pollution—but still much greater than in sediments deposited before the 1830s (0.7 ton) (Balogh et al. 2009).

To better understand the relationship between levels of lead in blood and feathers, we collected samples from both of these tissues from each eaglet in 2010. These data were not available for this report, but future analyses may provide correlations that will allow us to link levels of lead in feathers to thresholds known for blood.

Legacy contaminants

DDT/DDD/DDE
We expected few detections and very low levels of DDT because this pesticide was banned in North America more than 30 years before this study. However, DDT continues to enter the Great Lakes by atmospheric transport and deposition from regional sources, such as windblown sediments from abandoned manufacturing sites (Kannon et al. 2006), and global sources where it

49

is still used to control the spread of malaria (Roberts et al. 2000). We found quantifiable levels of DDT in plasma from nine eaglets - seven from Lake Superior and two from the Mississippi River. One nestling in 2009 on the upper portion of the MISS study area (Durnam Island) had 7.30 ug/L of DDT. This was four times greater than the next highest sample, and levels this high in bald eagles have not been reported in recent literature. The source is unknown, but an illegal release of DDT in the area cannot be ruled out.

According to USEPA the levels of total DDT (sum of DDT and its metabolites DDE and DDD) in Lake Superior lake trout (*Salvelinus namaycush*) have declined since 1977 and have remained below the Great Lakes Water Quality Agreement criteria of 1.0 $\mu g/g$ since 1989 (USEPA 2010). We found DDT in bald eagles from Lake Superior to be <2.0 ug/L and this was probably the result of dietary intake of contaminated fish and/or birds. Much of this contamination may come from outside of the region. For example, Giesy et al. (1994) used the ratio of DDE to DDT in fish above and below dams on rivers flowing into the Great Lakes to show that DDT in fish is primarily from long-range atmospheric transport and deposition.

We found that levels of DDD were often higher in eaglets from the Mississippi River study areas than in eaglets from Lake Superior, whereas the opposite was true for DDE. Both chemicals are metabolites of DDT, but they differ in that DDE exists entirely from the breakdown of DDT whereas DDD itself was used as an insecticide in the past (ATSDR 2002). Differences in source inputs, such as past use of DDD in agricultural areas of central Minnesota, and the chemical and physical properties of the two areas (e.g., water temperature, biological activity, very short versus long retention time) probably account for the differences we observed in these two metabolites. Very little comparative literature exists on DDD levels alone.

Levels of DDE were significantly higher in eaglets from the Apostle Islands and Lake Superior shoreline than in eaglets from the upper St. Croix River. Moreover, DDE was consistently highest in nestlings from the outer-most islands of the Apostles (all three years they were measured; Appendix D). The reason for this pattern on the Apostles is unknown but is likely related to food availability and magnification in the food web.

Kozie and Anderson (1991) reported that the relative percent of prey remains found under bald eagle nests on the Apostle Islands was 21% herring gull (*Larus argentatus*), 15.4% longnose sucker (*Catostomus catostomus*), and 13.5% burbot (*Lota lota*), with other fish and birds generally found in less than 6% of the collections. Burbot are fatty and long-lived fish (up to 22 years; McPhail 1997), factors associated with bioaccumulation of organochlorine compounds. Kozie and Anderson (1991) proposed that herring gulls are a major dietary source of DDE in bald eagles at APIS, and this relation was further supported by Dykstra et al. (2010). Herring gulls are top-level predators/scavengers in the Lake Superior food web, and blood concentrations of DDE have been positively correlated with trophic position (Elliott et al. 2009). Herring gull predation may also have contributed to the findings of Bowerman (2003) who found levels of DDE to be significantly higher in nestlings using the Great Lakes and Voyageurs National Park than those using interior lakes in Michigan and Minnesota. Predation on birds, including herring gulls, tends to be less frequent in inland eagle populations. At 80 bald eagle nests in inland Wisconsin, only 6% of the remains were of birds (P. Keasling and C. Sindelar, unpublished data cited in Kozie and Anderson 1991). To examine this relationship at APIS would require continuous monitoring of nests to document prey delivery, because collections of prey remains from under nests tend to be biased towards species that are not fully digested. A better approach would be to analyze ratios of stable isotopes (C and N) in eaglets and prey to examine how trophic position affects levels of contaminants in bald eagle nestlings at different study sites.

A recent analysis of our data combined with past data collected by the WDNR shows that DDE levels declined in nestling bald eagles on Lake Superior at a rate of about 3% per year from 1989 to 2009 (Dykstra et al. 2010), but the rate of decline has slowed (estimated at 5.2% between 1989 and 2001; Dykstra et al. 2005). Average productivity of bald eagles on the Great Lakes has increased since the lows in the 1960s and 1970s. We estimated average productivity well above the 0.7 young per occupied nest considered necessary for population stability (Sprunt et al. 1973) and above the 1.0 young per occupied nest considered representative of a healthy bald eagle population (Wiemeyer et al. 1984, Bowerman 2003). Yet in 2008 we found productivity in the APIS population to be just at the healthy population threshold and the mean productivity on the two Lake Superior study areas to be 1.2 young per occupied nest, still far below that observed for inland bald eagle populations - including those we monitored (1.6 - 2.0 young per occupied nest). This low productivity on Lake Superior is likely due to low food availability as a result of the lake being highly oligotrophic (unproductive). Dykstra et al. (1998, 2005) reported that prey delivery rates to eaglets in Lake Superior nests were significantly lower than at inland nests and may have been inadequate for growth of two young at some nests. By contrast, riverine nesting eagles have higher productivity when compared to eagles nesting on inland lakes in Wisconsin (M. Meyer, unpublished data).

Exposure to contaminants can be an added stressor to an eagle population stressed by limited food resources. Though DDE is slowly declining on the Great Lakes we found that about 50% of the nestlings we sampled at APIS (n = 19) still had more than 28 ug/L DDE in plasma, the threshold associated with a healthy population (Elliot and Harris 2001/2002). Moreover, APIS nestlings had DDE concentrations that were 1.5 times higher than adjacent Lake Superior south shore nestlings (Dykstra et al. 2010). We have no evidence of direct population-level effects from DDE, but sublethal effects on individuals with high concentrations cannot be ruled out.

PCBs

Elliott and Harris (2001/2002) estimated the threshold for significant impairment of bald eagle productivity (<0.7 young per occupied territory) to be 190 µg/kg of total PCBs in plasma. We found geometric mean levels of total PCBs in eaglet plasma were below this threshold at all study areas (highest geometric mean was 139 ug/L at L-SACN in 2006), suggesting that PCBs were not depressing reproductive rates from 2006-2009.

However, as with DDE, levels of PCBs in some individual nestlings exceeded this threshold level, and reproduction at individual nests near contaminant "hotspots" could have been affected. Concentrations at these nests are likely linked to local prey availability and/or selection by the adult eagles. Eagles preying on piscivorous birds or older aged predatory fish consume greater amounts of contaminants because of biomagnification through the food chain.

When combined with data from the WDNR our data support an estimated decline of 4.3% per year of total PCBs in plasma of bald eagle nestlings from the Great Lakes (Dykstra et al. 2010).

51

Others have reported similar declines of PCBs in Great Lakes water, sediments, and other biota (Bowerman et al. 2003, Carlson et al. 2010). Similar declines have also been reported for fish in the upper Mississippi River (Lee and Anderson 1998, Wiener and Sandheinrich 2010).

Differences in contaminant concentrations in the water, sediment, and biota among the four study areas may be attributed to differences in hydrology and potential source inputs. Lake Superior is cold, deep, oligotrophic, has a large watershed with slow turnover time (estimated at 191 years; Hites 2006), and receives much of its contaminant load from atmospheric deposition (Strachan and Eisenreich 1988). Contaminant concentrations in Lake Superior and its biota likely represent the slow recovery from the high levels of contamination of decades past. Elevated concentrations of total PCBs in the Mississippi River and some lower St. Croix River eaglets (compared to the Lake Superior eaglets) are likely due to industrial development. Wiener and Sandheinrich (2010), who summarized published information on the upper Mississippi River, showed that PCB levels in emergent female mayflies (*Hexagenia bilineata*) were greatest near industrialized areas, such as the Twin Cities. Such contamination low on the aquatic food web will be magnified to fish and higher trophic-level species, such as eagles.

Emerging contaminants of concern

PBDEs
PBDEs are a large group of chemicals (209 congeners) that are widely used to retard fire in a number of commercial products from plastics to textiles and foams. There are different formulations of these chemicals with the most common ones referred to as penta-, octa-, and deca-brominated flame retardants, relative to the number of bromine-carbon bonds. The PBDEs are chemically very similar to the PCBs.

The nine congeners we monitored are primarily in the penta-, and some in the octa-, formulations (Appendix A). These formulations have been under intense scrutiny because of their global occurrence in biological systems (Chen and Hale 2010), their persistence in the environment, the fact that they bioaccumulate in biota including humans, and because there is increasing evidence of toxicity (ATSDR 2004, Talsness 2008, Vonderheide et al. 2008). Moreover, past market demand for products with penta-PBDEs show that North America is the primary source/sink of these chemicals with global sales in 2003 estimated at 70,000 metric tons and North America consuming 98% in 1999 and 95% in 2001 (Hites 2004).

As a consequence of scientific and regulatory scrutiny, the European Union, Canada, and some States (California, Oregon, and Washington) have banned or have laws pending to ban the penta- and octa-PBDEs. Industry has, therefore, started phasing out these formulations. Some of these laws took effect just before or during this study and our results should be considered in this context. Though some industries may have decreased use prior to these bans, others may have increased production to use available stocks.

We found the highest levels of total PBDEs (sum of the nine congeners) in nestlings around Pig's Eye Lake in South St. Paul on the MISS study area and at a nest east of the city of Superior, Wisconsin, on Lake Superior. To the best of our knowledge these nests are the only ones immediately adjacent to waste disposal sites. As previously described above for lead contamination, Pig's Eye Lake is the site of decades of waste disposal and current wastewater treatment for the city of St. Paul. Similarly, the Lake Superior nest location is on the abandoned open-dump and within 1.5 km of the new landfill for the city of Superior. Both sites have readily available eagle prey that is high on the trophic food web, including a great blue heron (*Ardea herodias*) rookery at Pig's Eye Lake and a gull colony near the Superior, Wisconsin, site. This connection is speculative because we did not study the food habits of sampled eaglets. However, PBDEs are known to leach from plastics and textiles from a number of commercial and household products found in landfills (Kim et al. 2006). And elevated levels of PBDEs are well documented in gulls (Norstrom et al. 2002) and great blue herons (Custer et al. 2009, 2010).

We found significant differences in the spatial patterns of PBDE congeners among the six study areas. Geometric mean levels of all five congeners, compared with mixed effects models, were significantly lower in eaglets from the more remote upper St. Croix Riverway, slightly higher in the lower St. Croix, and usually highest in eaglets from the Mississippi River and Lake Superior study areas, though the latter two varied depending on the congener.

Others have also found high levels near urban areas. Strandberg et al. (2001) found the sum of eight PBDEs in the air around Chicago to be 3-fold higher than those at Sleeping Bear Dunes in northeastern Lake Michigan and 10-fold higher than those on the Keweenaw Peninsula in southcentral Lake Superior. This pattern is also evident in Great Lakes bottom sediments where studies have found that levels of PBDEs are highest near human population centers, and that elevated levels in more rural areas can be linked to prevailing wind patterns away from these urban areas (Song et al. 2005).

We found that PBDE congeners #47, #99, and #100 accounted for the bulk of the total PBDE volume (84%) in eaglet plasma with 53%, 16%, and 15% respectively. The high proportion of #47 was also found in bald eagle nestlings sampled on the Pacific Northwest coast of North America, where investigators estimated it accounted for half of the total PBDE volume (McKinney et al. 2006). In the air around the Great Lakes, Strandberg et al. (2001) found that PBDE #47 accounted for 50-65% and PBDE #99 about 35-40%, whereas the remaining five congeners together totaled less than 10%. Moreover, they concluded that this composition remained relatively uniform across the Great Lakes. Similar ratios were found in sediments from Lakes Michigan and Huron (Song et al. 2005) and lake trout in Lake Ontario (Ismail et al. 2009). Interestingly, the commercial penta-flame retardants used in textiles as an additive to polyurethane foams has a congener composition similar to what we found in bald eagle plasma. There is variation in commercial mixtures, but the major PBDE congeners in commercial mixtures are #47, # 99, and #100 (the so called penta-BDEs) with #47 and #99 accounting for approximately 75% of the total mass (WHO 1994).

In a summary of information on PBDEs in the Great Lakes, Hites (2006b) concluded that PBDEs (most studies measured the penta- and octa- formulations) have increased greatly in all media on the Great Lakes (from sediments to fish and birds) since 1980, with a doubling time of three to five years, but that there are signs that concentrations are leveling off. Specific to our study areas on Lake Superior, Dykstra et al. (2005) sampled five eaglets on Lake Superior in 2001 for the same nine PBDE congeners that we measured. They found the geometric mean of total PBDEs in eaglet plasma to be 8.40 *ug*/kg. In 2006 we sampled eight nestlings at APIS with a geometric mean of 14.1 *ug*/L, which is 1.6 times higher than the 2001 estimate. Sample sizes are admittedly small and we did not sample from the same nests, however, this increase in five years fits well with other studies across the Great Lakes and globally (see Chen and Hale 2010 for a global review of PBDEs in birds). To further investigate this apparent increase, in 2007 we sampled both APIS and the remaining Lake Superior south shore (LSSS study area) including all nesting territories sampled in 2001 by Dykstra et al. (2005). We estimated a combined geometric mean of 11.3 ug/L (n = 12). In 2008 we sampled five nests at APIS and four nests near the APIS boundary in the LSSS study area. The geometric mean level of the combined sample was 6.50 ug/L. These data suggest that the penta- and octa- formulations of PBDEs increased in bald eagle nestlings from 2001 to 2006 and have begun to decline, in general agreement with the findings of others in a variety of media on the Great Lakes (Hites 2006).

PFCs

Perfluorinated compounds (PFCs) have the unique chemical properties of repelling both water and oil, which makes them useful for many products. The number and variety of products that incorporate PFCs in their manufacture is enormous, including drugs, anesthetics, chemotherapeutic agents, pesticides, refrigerants, and polymers such as Teflon™ and Gortex™.

The primary PFCs of interest during this study were PFOS and PFOA. These two analytes are ubiquitous in the environment and have come under intense scientific and regulatory scrutiny (Giesy and Kannan 2001, Kannan et al. 2006). Most other investigators have also focused on PFOS and PFOA; hence there is very little published literature on the chemical properties, bioaccumulation factors, sources, and fates of the other PFC analytes. This, combined with our limited data on 14 of the analytes we monitored (four years of data on PFOS and PFOA; only two years on the other 14), limits the following discussion primarily to PFOS and PFOA.

The bond between carbon and fluorine is one of the strongest known among organic compounds and as a result many PFCs are highly persistent in the environment (Moody et al. 2002, MDH 2010). However, the adsorption, solubility, and atmospheric transport of the various PFCs differ greatly. Higgins and Luthy (2006) found that the carbon chain length in PFCs had a major effect on sorption and that PFOS tended to bind more readily to sediment than PFOA. Organic carbon content, pH, dissolved calcium, and other environmental conditions of soil and water can also affect adsorption. In a review of the bioaccumulative properties of PFCs, Conder et al. (2008) found that the longer chained PFCs, which include PFOS, had greater potential to accumulate in living organisms. Some of the more volatile PFCs, such as PFOA, are known to reach remote locations around the world where they can metabolize to form PFOS (Martin et al. 2002).

We found PFOS to be the most prevalent PFC in bald eagle nestling plasma, making up over 50% of the total PFC load by volume. Similar findings have been noted by others in water, algae, amphipods, freshwater mussels, crayfish, and several fish species in the Great Lakes food web (Kannan et al. 2005), in fish from lakes and streams of the upper Midwest (Ye et al. 2008a, Ye et al. 2008b, Delinsky et al. 2010, Nakayama et al. 2010), and in human blood (Kubwabo et al. 2004, Olsen et al. 2008). Kannan et al. (2005) showed that PFOS has a high capacity to biomagnify in food webs with an approximate overall bioaccumulation factor (BAF) of 1,000 in lower trophic-level organisms (water to: algae, amphipods, mussels, and crayfish), increasing to 2,400 in the round goby (*Neogobius melanostomus*; water to whole body), and increasing another 10- to 20-fold from round goby to Chinook salmon (*Oncorhynchus tshawytscha*; whole goby to salmon liver). Direct relations between PFOS contamination in water and the levels found in higher organisms may be confounded, however, because some PFCs are metabolized by organisms with PFOS as the end product (Tomy et al. 2004). Interestingly, the Minnesota Department of Health (MDH) has sampled soils, ground water, surface water, private wells, and aquifers around 3M disposal sites and has often found that the PFC with the highest concentration is PFBA (MDH 2010), an analyte that was negligible in bald eagle plasma in our study (<1% by volume). Yet, the MDH studies did not quantify PFDS, an analyte we found in bald eagles at concentrations second only to PFOS on Mississippi River sites. The reasons for the relatively high ratio of PFDS in eaglets from the Mississippi River are unknown.

When all four years of data are considered, we found the U-SACN and LSSS study areas had the lowest concentrations of PFOS (<600 *ug*/L). Concentrations of PFOS were substantially higher on the L-SACN study area, especially below St. Croix Falls, and on the MISS study area below the confluence of the Minnesota and Mississippi Rivers. The highest level we found exceeded 2400 *ug*/L PFOS in plasma of a nestling on the Vermillion River bottoms southeast of Hastings, Minnesota. These results are comparable to those of Kannan and Giesy (2001) who reported PFOS levels to range from <1 *ug*/L to 2570 *ug*/L (mean 360 *ug*/L) in plasma from 26 bald eagle nestlings sampled between 1991-1993 across the upper Midwestern United States. We know of no other data on PFOS levels in plasma of bald eagle nestlings for comparison. Giesy et al. (2006) summarized data from a variety of organisms across the Great Lakes region and consistently found PFOS at much higher levels than PFOA in higher taxa: reptiles, amphibians, mammals, birds, and fish. This relationship was less prevalent for water, invertebrates and benthic algae.

The "hotspots" we found on the Mississippi and St. Croix rivers were bracketed upstream and downstream by nestlings with much lower levels of PFOS, suggesting a source with limited downstream transport (see Figure 19). High levels of PFOS were not surprising in the reach of river below South St. Paul where 3M has manufactured and disposed of PFCs from the 1950s through 2000. Less easily explained were the high levels at two nests on the lower St. Croix River. We hypothesize that the high concentrations in some eaglets are due in part to an accumulation of PFOS in sediments and the addition of a trophic-step in the eagle's diet. Both the Pig's Eye Lake area on the Mississippi River and the hot spots on the lower St. Croix River have backwater sloughs where sediments settle. Both areas also have great blue heron rookeries. PFOS readily binds to sediments (Giesy et al. 2006), and herons often feed in backwater sloughs where they can accumulate these contaminants from their prey. Custer et al. (2009, 2010) has shown that great blue herons accumulate PFOS to high levels, and bald eagles are known to prey on young heron (Norman et al. 1989).

While the bulk of the Mississippi River PFOS is probably from past disposal practices by 3M, the source of PFOS on the lower St. Croix River is less evident. A number of industries located in the vicinity of St. Croix Falls, Wisconsin, and Taylors Falls, Minnesota, may have used PFOS or precursor analytes. For example, the MDH and the Minnesota Pollution Control Agency (MPCA) found high levels of PFOS in wastewater effluent below some cities with chrome plating industries (MDH and MPCA, St. Paul, Minnesota, unpublished data).

The PFC analytes PFDS, PFHpS, and PFHxS showed patterns similar to PFOS in eaglet plasma, albeit at substantially lower concentrations. Of these, PFDS was second only to PFOS and contributed 26% of the PFC load in nestlings on the Mississippi River study areas, but only 1% on the Lake Superior study areas (2008 and 2009 estimates). We found little information on the chemistry, sources, transport, and environmental fate of PFDS and the other analytes in this group.

By contrast we found that PFOA, PFuDA, PFTrDA and PFNA were at their highest levels in nestlings from Lake Superior. PFOA, the analyte of high interest in this group, made up $\leq 1\%$ on average of total PFCs by volume. Though proportionally small, geometric mean levels of PFOA were highest in eaglets from Lake Superior compared to the other study areas. This was most notable in nestlings from the outer islands of APIS, though one nestling on the lower St. Croix River (at High Bridge) reached the highest level we measured at 10 ug/L. Giesy and Kannan (2006) showed that PFOA has relatively low biomagnification properties, citing others who estimated BAFs of 4.0 for PFOA in juvenile rainbow trout (*Oncorhynchus mykiss*) compared to 1,100 for PFOS. PFOA is also more water soluble than PFOS and has a longer half-life in the atmosphere (92 years; Giesy et al. 2006). Major manufactures of PFOA include 3M in our study area and DuPont Corporation's Teflon™ production facility in Parkersburg, West Virginia (Karstadt 2007), but others are scattered globally. Simcik and Dorweiler (2005) used ratios of polluted urban waters to unpolluted remote waters to argue that proximate source of PFCs in Lake Michigan was wastewater treatment plants (WWTPs). This finding was further refined by Scott et al. (2010) who examined surface waters, tributary inputs, and effluent from WWTPs. They found PFOA to be the predominant PFC (0.07 to 1.2 ng/L) in surface waters of Lake Superior and concluded that WWTPs increased concentrations of PFOA up to 20-fold more than intake water and that precipitation accounted for 35% of the annual input (Scott et al. 2010).

A general conclusion from these studies may be that about 35% of the PFOA in Lake Superior is from atmospheric deposition and 65% is from water-borne inflow, a large portion of which is from WWTPs on the lake or on a tributary to the lake. We expect both PFOA and PFOS levels to begin declining across our study areas, given that 3M, DuPont and seven other major producers of this chemical have agreed to phase-out production by 2015, and both 3M and DuPont have met or exceeded their 2010 goals (MDH 2010, personal communication with DuPont public information officer, respectively).

The other PFC analytes that were significantly higher in Lake Superior versus the Mississippi River were PFuDA, PFTrDA and PFNA, and we have no information on the sources or chemical properties of these analytes. PFTDA and PFDoA were also measured at higher concentrations on Lake Superior, but these measurements were not statistically significant. Overall, Lake Superior had a distribution of PFCs that was less skewed towards PFOS compared to the Mississippi River. This probably reflects the greater capacity of Lake Superior to receive and retain globally generated airborne contaminants while the Mississippi River tends to carry contaminants from more regional sources.

We found that levels of PFOS and five other PFCs increased significantly with the age and weight of the sampled eaglets. Eaglet age influenced PFOS levels more than weight, but the reverse was true for PFHxS, PFNA, PFTeDA, PFTrDA, and PFuDA. However, both age and weight of eaglets were highly correlated (r = 0.79), so both factors were contributory. On average PFOS levels increased in eaglets at a rate of 3% per day while the other five analytes increased by 23% to 35% for each kilogram of body weight. These findings are supportive of the high bioaccumulation factor found by others for PFOS and suggest that the other five PFCs share in this property. The age of our eaglets varied by as much as 50 days and the weights varied by 3.5

kg; hence, a two- to four-fold difference in levels of these six PFCs might be expected during routine monitoring of eaglets. We took these factors into account by including them in mixed effects models in our analyses and we caution that others should consider them when designing programs and comparing among study areas and through time.

Four analytes, PFOA, PFDA, PFDS, and PFHpS did not vary significantly with either weight or age. Again, this is supportive of the low bioaccumulation factors found by others for PFOA and suggests the other three in this group have low potential for bioaccumulation as well.

A number of studies have documented toxicity of PFOS and PFOA in laboratory animals (Betts 2007, MDH 2010). At high concentrations, they can alter the production of thyroid hormones, cause liver damage, suppress the immune system, and are carcinogenic (MDH 2010). But the toxicity of PFOS and PFOA has not been directly measured for top level predatory birds. Newsted et al. (2005) calculated a toxicity reference value (TRV) of 1700 ug/L PFOS in serum, which is a conservative number to be protective of avian species. The authors used USEPA Great Lakes Initiative methodology (USEPA 1995) incorporating uncertainty factors for observed effects, duration of exposure, and intertaxa relationships. The resulting TRV was based on acute and chronic dietary exposures to PFOS on bobwhite quail (*Colinus virginianus*) reproduction and extrapolated to the characteristics of a trophic level IV fish-eating bird such as the bald eagle. Newsted et al. (2005) reasoned that the resulting TRV incorporates contributions of PFOS from both aquatic and terrestrial pathways. We are not aware of any TRVs for PFOA or other PFCs in serum.

Giesy et al. (2006) further explored the potential toxicity of PFOS in wildlife and calculated a no observable adverse effects level (NOAEL) of 30,500 ug/L for bird serum. The authors further concluded that current concentrations of PFOS in birds - and our data fit within these levels - are within a factor of 10 of the threshold likely to cause ecologically relevant effects. Indeed our highest measured concentration was less than this NOAEL by a factor of 12. Moreover, none of our study areas had geometric mean levels of PFOS exceeding the TRV of 1700 ug/L. The L-SACN and MISS study areas had the highest levels with 1580 ug/L and 1250 ug/L respectively. We found two nestlings at L-SACN (8.7%) and three at MISS (5.5%) that exceeded 1700 ug PFOS/L, but there were no exceedences in the other study areas. We found no measurable effects on either the individual or population level, though our measurements were limited to gross external features and overall productivity.

PFC concentrations in eaglets appear to have declined from 2006 through 2009 in at least the Mississippi River and lower St. Croix study areas. We will continue monitoring PFC concentrations through 2011, adding two years of observations to this data set. Temporal trends will be analyzed at the conclusion of the 2011 field season.

Conclusions and Management Implications

The NPS Great Lakes Inventory and Monitoring Network and its partners have implemented this monitoring program to assist national parks and other resource managers in the upper Midwest to better understand the spatial patterns and trends of targeted environmental contaminants. This report covers the beginning of this program, from 2006 through 2009. Data will continue to be collected in 2010 and 2011 and thereafter at two-year intervals. Conclusions and recommendations made here are subject to change as we learn more about the patterns and trends of these contaminants and the complex systems they affect.

At this juncture we make the following observations and recommendations:

1. Bald eagle productivity in the region has increased dramatically from lows in the 1960s and 1970s and is at or above levels considered necessary for a healthy population. Productivity is highest on the Mississippi River and lowest on Lake Superior, with the St. Croix River nearly spanning this gradient. The lower productivity observed on Lake Superior is likely due to lower food availability compared to the other study areas.

2. We have no evidence that the contaminants being monitored are adversely affecting bald eagle productivity at the population level. However, some contaminants may exert sublethal and occasionally lethal effects on individuals at "hot spots" where concentrations in eaglets were high. Current research on the effects of some contaminants on brain chemistry of eagles may provide answers in the coming years.

3. Mercury levels in biota including bald eagles have been steadily declining in the region, but these trends could reverse. Increasing concentrations in some biota, together with the relatively high levels we measured in eaglets from the upper St. Croix River, indicates that continued monitoring of this pervasive contaminant is warranted.

4. The National Park Service and its partners should determine threshold levels for mercury in eagle nestling feathers. Cooperative work with the University of Michigan on the effects of mercury on neurochemistry of eagles holds promise for this need and should be continued.

5. There were five instances of elevated lead exposure in bald eagle nestlings, four of which occurred in eaglets from Pig's Eye Lake on Pool 2 of the Upper Mississippi River. We recommend further research into the levels of lead in sediments, soils, and other media in this area for potential remediation. Continued monitoring of lead levels at one nest on the lower St. Croix is warranted (High Bridge Island).

6. The relationship between lead levels in feathers and known toxicity thresholds in blood are unclear. We should measure lead in both blood and feathers in future years to explore this relationship with the hope of developing a threshold for lead in feathers.

7. DDT and its metabolites DDD and DDE continue to linger more than 30 years after DDT was banned in North America. This is particularly evident in Lake Superior, where eaglets continue to bioaccumulate DDE, and occasionally DDT, from the food web. This was especially evident for DDE on the outer islands of the Apostle Islands. We propose, as have others, that this is due to an additional trophic step in the food chain in this area (such as older fish with higher lipid content and/or a higher percentage of piscivorous

birds in the diet), but this should be researched more thoroughly with sampling of sediments and prey in areas with consistently high DDE levels. One extremely high concentration of DDT in a nestling on Durnam Island in the Mississippi National River and Recreation Area warrants further investigation from local authorities for potential illegal use.

8. The Great Lakes Network and its partners should seek funding to analyze stable isotopes (C and N) in eaglets and/or prey to assess how trophic position affects levels of contaminants in bald eagle nestlings.

9. Though levels are still elevated in some areas, our data in combination with a longer data set from the Wisconsin Department of Natural Resources, shows that DDE declined in eaglets on Lake Superior at a rate of 3% annually between 1989 and 2008. There is evidence this trend is slowing, however, probably due to the capacity of Lake Superior to retain contaminants in its cold, deep, oligotrophic waters. Similar trend data were not available for our other study areas, but the literature suggests this decline is regional.

10. In combination with a longer data set from the Wisconsin Department of Natural Resources, our data show that PCBs declined in bald eagle nestlings on Lake Superior at an annual rate of 4.3% between 1989 and 2008. Similar data were not available for the other study areas, but as with DDE, the literature suggests that this trend is regional. We found average levels to be below known thresholds in all study areas, though some nestlings, particularly those near urban centers or that feed on higher trophic-level prey, may suffer sublethal effects of PCB exposure.

11. The penta- and octa- formulations of PBDEs appear to have increased from the 2001 to our first sampling in 2006, but average levels have since dropped on Lake Superior. This apparent increase and decline coincides with industry use and subsequent international bans and phasing-out of these flame retardant formulations. We will begin monitoring the deca-formulations in 2010 to determine if they are increasing as a result industry switching to them. There are no thresholds set for PBDEs in bald eagles, but a cooperative effort with the University of Michigan holds some promise for determining sublethal effects of PBDEs on eagle brain chemistry, and this effort should be continued.

12. We found high levels of PFCs, especially PFOS, in bald eagle nestlings on the lower Mississippi and lower St. Croix Rivers. Due to changing numbers of PFCs measured during this program and too few years of data we did not evaluate trends in these chemicals. Preliminary evaluations of PFOA and PFOS, however, suggest that these PFCs are declining on the Mississippi River - coinciding with the phase-out of production by 3M. It is likely that the high levels we observed are associated with accumulations in sediments and subsequent biomagnification in the local food web. We expect these chemicals to decline post phase-out, however, some are highly persistent and could linger for decades. Hence continued monitoring is highly recommended.

13. Statistical differences in contaminant burdens among study areas provide insights into the sources, mechanisms of transport, and magnification through the food web. Generally, contaminants associated with industry and municipal waste (PCBs, PBDEs, PFCs, and to a lesser extent, lead) were highest in bald eagle nestlings near large population centers. Lake Superior, however, receives a wide array of pollutants from global sources through air deposition and retains them for longer periods of time; hence nestlings in remote

islands had high levels of some industrial contaminants. These patterns of distribution were further complicated by apparent magnification in the food web at individual nest territories where high trophic-level prey was available.

14. Much of the background levels of lead in eaglets are probably from legacy use of alkyl lead in gasoline, but we found elevated levels in some nestlings near sites with contaminated soils and sediments from industrial or municipal waste.

15. There is great potential for public education with the results from this program. Bald eagles are a species of high interest to the public, and they can serve as a biosentinel to foster greater awareness of the hazards of toxic substances in the environment. Resource managers and educators should adopt programs, such as "Get the Lead Out," and provide information on hazardous waste disposal and proper use of burn barrels.

16. The relationships among environmental contaminants and climate, water quality, and land use in and around parks should be examined more thoroughly in future analyses.

17. Following data analysis of samples collected in 2011 a thorough analysis of trends for each contaminant should be completed.

Literature Cited

ATSDR (Agency for Toxic Substances and Disease Registry). 2002. Toxicological profile for DDT, DDE, and DDD. U.S. Department of Health and Human Services report available at http://www.atsdr.cdc.gov/toxprofiles/tp35.pdf.

ATSDR. 2004. Public health statement: Polybrominated diphenyl ethers. U.S. Department of Health and Human Services report available at http://www.atsdr.cdc.gov/tfacts68-pbde.pdf (accessed 9 August 2010).

Balogh, S. J., E. B. Swain, and Y. H. Nollet. 2008. Characteristics of mercury speciation in Minnesota rivers and streams. Environmental Pollution 154:3-11.

Balogh, S. J., L. D. Triplett, D. R. Engstrom, and Y. H. Nollet. 2010. Historical trace metal loading to a large river recorded in the sediments of Lake St. Croix, USA. Journal of Paleolimnology 44:517-530.

Betts, K. S. 2007. Perfluoroalkyl acids: What is the evidence telling us? Environmental Health Perspectives 115:251-256.

Beyer, W. N., and J. P. Meador, editors. 2011. Environmental Contaminants in Biota: Interpreting Tissue Concentrations, 2nd edition. CRC Press/Taylor and Francis, Boca Raton, Florida.

Bhavsar, S. P., S. B. Gewurtz, D. J. McGoldrick, M. J. Keir, and S. M. Backus. 2010. Changes in mercury levels in Great Lakes fish between 1970s and 2007. Environmental Science and Technology 44:3273-3279.

Bowerman, W. W., IV. 1993. Regulation of bald eagle (*Haliaeetus leucocephalus*) productivity in the Great Lakes basin: An ecological and toxicological approach. Dissertation. Michigan State University, East Lansing, Michigan.

Bowerman, W. W., T. J. Kubiak, J. B. Holt, D. L. Evans, R. G. Eckstein, C. R. Sindelar, D. A. Best, and K. D. Kozie. 1994. Observed abnormalities in mandibles of bald eagles (*Haliaeetus leucocephalus*). Bulletin of Environmental Contamination and Toxicology 53:450-475.

Bowerman, W. W., D. A. Best, J. P. Giesy, M. C. Shieldcastle, M. W. Meyer, S. Postupalsky, and J. G. Sikarskie. 2003. Associations between regional differences in polychlorinated biphenyls and dichlorodiphenyldichloroethylene in blood of nestling bald eagles and reproductive productivity. Environmental Toxicology and Chemistry 22:371-376.

Bortolotti, G. 1984. Criteria for determining age and sex of nestling bald eagles. Journal of Field Ornithology 55:467-481.

Braune, B. M., P. M. Outridge, A. T. Fisk, D. C. G. Muir, P. A. Helm, K. Hobbs, P. F. Hoekstra, Z. A. Kuzyk, M. Kwan, R. J. Letcher, W. L. Lockhart, and others. 2005. Persistent organic pollutants and mercury in marine biota of the Canadian Arctic: An overview of spatial and temporal trends. Science of the Total Environment 351–352:4-56.

Brigham, M. E., D. A. Wentz, G. R. Aiken, and D. P. Krabbenhoft. 2009. Mercury cycling in stream ecosystems. 1. Water column chemistry and transport. Environmental Science and Technology 43:2720-2725.

Burnham, K. P., and D. R. Anderson. 1998. Model Selection and Inference: A Practical Information-theoretic Approach. Springer-Verlag, New York.

Burger, J., and M. Gochfeld. 2009. Comparison of arsenic, cadmium, chromium, lead, manganese, mercury and selenium in feathers in bald eagle (*Haliaeetus leucocephalus*), and comparison with common eider (*Somateria mollissima*), glaucous-winged gull (*Larus glaucescens*), pigeon guillemot (*Cepphus columba*), and tufted puffin (*Fratercula cirrhata*) from the Aleutian Chain of Alaska. Environmental Monitoring and Assessment 152:357–367.

Bush, B., J. Snow, and R. Koblintz. 1984. Polychlorobiphenyl (PCB) congeners, p,p'-DDE and hexachlorobenzene in maternal and fetal cord blood from mothers in upstate New York. Archives of Environmental Contamination and Toxicology 15:517-527.

Carlson D. L., D. S. De Vault, and D. L. Swackhamer. 2010. On the rate of decline of persistent organic contaminants in lake trout (*Salvelinus namaycush*) from the Great Lakes, 1970-2003. Environmental Science and Technology 44:2004-2010.

Chasar, L. C., B. C. Scudder, A. R. Stewart, A. H. Bell, and G. R. Aiken. 2009. Mercury cycling in stream ecosystems. 3. Trophic dynamics and methylmercury bioaccumulation. Environmental Science and Technology 43:2733-2739.

Chen, D., and R. C. Hale. 2010. A global review of polybrominated diphenyl ether flame retardant contamination in birds. Environment International 36:800-811.

Christensen, V. G., S. P. Wente, M. B. Sandheinrich, and M. E. Brigham. 2006. Spatial variation in fish-tissue mercury concentrations in the St. Croix River basin, Minnesota and Wisconsin, 2004. U.S. Department of Interior, U.S. Geological Survey Scientific Investigations Report 2006-5063.

Conder, J. M., R. A. Hoke, W. De Wolf, M. H. Russell, and R. C. Buck. 2008. Are PFCs bioaccumulative? A critical review and comparison with regulatory criteria and persistent lipophilic compounds. Environmental Science and Technology 42:995-1003.

Custer, T. W., N. H. Golden, and B. A. Rattner. 2008. Element patterns in feathers of nestling black-crowned night-herons, *Nycticorax nycticorax* L., from four colonies in Delaware, Maryland, and Minnesota. Bulletin of Environmental Contamination and Toxicology 81:147-151.

Custer, T. W., K. Kannan, K. L. Tao, A. R. Saxena, and B. Route. 2009. Perfluorinated compounds and polybrominated diphenyl ethers in great blue heron eggs from Indiana Dunes National Lakeshore, Indiana. Journal of Great Lakes Research 35:401–405.

Custer, T. W., K. Kannan, L. Tao, S. H. Yun, and A. Trowbridge. 2010. Perfluorinated compounds and polybrominated diphenyl ethers in great blue heron eggs from three colonies on the Mississippi River, Minnesota. Waterbirds 33:86-95

Delinsky A. D., M. J. Strynar, P. J. McCann, J. L. Varns, L. McMillan, S. F. Nakayama, and A. B. Lindstrom. 2010. Geographical distribution of perfluorinated compounds in fish from Minnesota lakes and rivers. Environmental Science & Technology 44:2549-2554.

DeSorbo, C. R., and D. C. Evers. 2007. Evaluating exposure of Maine's bald eagle population to mercury: Assessing impacts on productivity and spatial exposure patterns. Report BRI 2007-02. BioDiversity Research Institute, Gorham, Maine.

Dykstra, C. J. R. 1995. Effects of contaminants, food availability and weather on the reproductive rate of Lake Superior bald eagles (*Haliaeetus leucocephalus*). Dissertation. University of Wisconsin-Madison, Madison, Wisconsin.

Dykstra, C. R., M. W. Meyer, D. K. Warnke, W. H. Karasov, D. E. Andersen, W. W. Bowerman, and J. P. Giesy. 1998. Low reproductive rates of Lake Superior bald eagles: Low food delivery rates or environmental contaminants? Journal of Great Lakes Research 24:32-44.

Dykstra, C. R., M. W. Meyer, P. Rasmussen, and D. K. Warnke. 2005. Contaminant concentrations and reproductive rate of Lake Superior bald eagles, 1989-2001. Journal of Great Lakes Research 31:227-235.

Dykstra, C. R., W. T. Route, M. W. Meyer, and P. W. Rasmussen. 2010. Contaminant concentrations in bald eagles nesting on Lake Superior, the upper Mississippi River, and the St. Croix River. Journal of Great Lakes Research 36:561-569.

Eisler, R. 1987. Mercury hazards to fish, wildlife and invertebrates: A synoptic review. U.S. Fish and Wildlife Service Biological Report 85 (1.10).

Elliot, J. E., and M. L. Harris. 2001/2002. An ecotoxicological assessment of chlorinated hydrocarbon effects on bald eagle populations. Reviews in Toxicology 4:1-60.

Elliot, K. H., L. S. Cesh, J. A. Dooley, R. J. Letcher, and J. E. Elliot. 2009. PCBs and DDE, but not PBDEs, increase with trophic level and marine input in nestling bald eagles. Science of the Total Environment 407:3867-3875.

Evers, D. C. 2005. Mercury connections: The extent and effects of mercury pollution in northeastern North America. BioDiversity Research Institute, Gorham, Maine.

Evers, D. C., O. P. Lane, L. Savoy, and W. Goodale. 2004. Assessing the impacts of methylmercury on piscivorous wildlife using a wildlife criterion value based on the common loon, 1998-2003. Report BRI 2004-05 submitted to the Maine Department of Environmental Protection. BioDiversity Research Institute, Gorham, Maine.

Evers, D. C., N. M. Burgess, L. Champoux, B. Hoskins, A. Major, W. M. Goodale, R. J. Taylor, R. Poppenga, and T. Daigle. 2005. Patterns and interpretation of mercury exposure in freshwater avian communities in northeastern North America. Ecotoxicology 14:193-221.

Fevold, B. M., M. W. Meyer, P. W. Rasmussen, and S. A. Temple. 2003. Bioaccumulation patterns and temporal trends of mercury exposure in Wisconsin common loons. Ecotoxicology 12:83-93.

Fernie, K. J., and R. J. Letcher. 2010. Historical contaminants, flame retardants, and halogenated phenolic compounds in peregrine falcon (*Falco peregrinus*) nestlings in the Canadian Great Lakes basin. Environmental Science and Technology 44:3520-3526.

Finkelstein, M. E., D. George, S. Scherbinski, R. Gwiazda, M. Johnson, J. Burnett, J. Brandt, S. Lawrey, A. P. Pessier, M. Clark, J. Wynne, and others. 2010. Feather lead concentrations and ^{207}Pb/^{206}Pb ratios reveal lead exposure history of California condors (*Gymnogyps californianus*). Environmental Science and Technology 44:2639-2647.

Friend, M., and D. O. Trainer. 1970. Some effects of sublethal levels of insecticides on vertebrates. Journal of Wildlife Diseases 6:335-342.

Gerrard, J. M., and G. R. Bortolotti. 1988. The Bald Eagle. Smithsonian Institution, Washington, D.C.

Giesy, J. P., D. A. Verbrugge, R. A. Othout, W. W. Bowerman, M. A. Mora, P. D. Jones, J. L. Newsted, C. Vandervoort, S. N, Heaton, R. J. Aulerich, S. J. Bursian, and others. 1994. Contaminants in fishes from Great Lakes-influenced sections and above dams of three Michigan rivers. I: Concentrations of organochlorine insecticides, polychlorinated biphenyls, dioxin equivalents, and mercury. Archives of Environmental Contamination and Toxicology 27:201-212.

Giesy, J. P., and K. Kannan. 2001. Global distribution of perfluorooctane sulfonate in wildlife. Environmental Science and Technology 35:1339-1342.

Giesy, J. P., S. A. Maybury, J. W. Martin, K. Kannan, P. D. Jones, J. L. Newstad, and K. Coady. 2006. Perfluorinated compounds in the Great Lakes. Pages 391-438 *in* R. A. Hites, editor. The handbook of environmental chemistry: Persistent organic pollutants in the Great Lakes. Springer-Verlag, Berlin and Heidelberg, Germany.

Grieb, T. M., G. L. Bowie, C. T. Driscoll, S. P. Gloss, C. L. Schofield, and D. B. Porcella. 2009. Factors affecting mercury accumulation in fish in the upper Michigan peninsula. Environmental Toxicology and Chemistry 9:919-930.

Hennes, S. K. 1985. Lead shot ingestion and lead residues in migrant bald eagles at the Lac Qui Parle Wildlife Management Area, Minnesota. Thesis. University of Minnesota, St. Paul, Minnesota.

Helsel, D. R. 2005. Nondetects and Data Analysis: Statistics for Censored Environmental Data. Wiley, New Jersey.

Helsel, D. R. 2009. Summing nondetects: Incorporating low-level contaminants in risk assessment. Integrated Environmental Assessment and Management 6:1-6.

Higgins, C. P., and R. G. Luthy. 2006. Sorption of perfluorinated surfactants on sediments. Environmental Science and Technology 40: 7251-7256.

Hites, R. A. 2004. Polybrominated diphenyl ethers in the environment and people: A meta-analysis of concentrations. Environmental Science and Technology 38:945-956.

Hites, R. A. 2006. Persistent organic pollutants in the Great Lakes: An overview. Pages 1-12 *in* R. A. Hites, editor. The handbook of environmental chemistry: Persistent organic pollutants in the Great Lakes. Springer-Verlag, Berlin and Heidelberg, Germany.

Hoffman, D. J., B. A. Rattner, G. A. Burton, Jr., and J. Cairns, Jr., editors. 2003. Handbook of Ecotoxicology, 2nd edition. CRC Press, Boca Raton, Florida.

Hoffman, K., T. F. Webster, M. G. Weisskopf, J. Weinberg, and V. M. Vieira. 2010. Exposure to polyfluoroalkyl chemicals and attention deficit/hyperactivity disorder in U.S. children 12-15 years of age. Environmental Health Perspectives 118:1762-1767.

Hooper, S. W., C. A. Pettigrew, and G. Sayler. 1990. Ecological fate, effects and prospects for elimination of environmental polychlorinated biphenyls (PCBs). Environmental Toxicology and Chemistry 9:655-667.

Hornbuckle, K. C., D. L. Carlson, D. L. Swackhamer, J. E. Baker, and S. J. Eisenreich. 2005. Polychlorinated biphenyls in the Great Lakes. Pages 13-70 *in* R. A. Hites, editor. The handbook of environmental chemistry: Persistent organic pollutants in the Great Lakes. Springer-Verlag, Berlin and Heidelberg, Germany.

Hrabik, T. R., and C. J. Watras. 2002. Recent declines in mercury concentration in a freshwater fishery: Isolating the effects of de-acidification and decreased atmospheric mercury deposition in Little Rock Lake. Science of the Total Environment 297:229-237.

Hudson, R. M., R. K. Tucker, and M. A. Haegele. 1984. Handbook of toxicity of pesticides to wildlife. U. S. Department of Interior, Fish and Wildlife Service. Resource Publication 153.

Hurley, J. P., J. M. Benoit, C. L. Babiarz, M. M. Shafer, A. W. Andren, J. R. Sullivan, R. Hammond, and D. A. Webb. 1995. Influences of watershed characteristics on mercury levels in Wisconsin rivers. Environmental Science and Technology 29:1867-1875.

Ikonomou, M. G., S. Rayne, and R. F. Addison. 2002. Exponential increases of the brominated flame retardants, polybrominated diphenyl ethers, in the Canadian arctic from 1981 to 2000. Environmental Science and Technology 36:1886-1892.

Ismail, N., S. B. Gewurtz, K. Pleskach, D. M. Whittle, P. A. Helm, C. H. Marvin, and G. T. Tomy. 2009. Brominated and chlorinated flame retardants in Lake Ontario, Canada, lake trout (*Salvelinus namaycush*) between 1979 and 2004 and possible influences of food-web changes. Environmental Toxicology and Chemistry 28:910-920.

Jagoe, C. H., A. L. Bryan, Jr., H. A. Brant, and T. M. Murphy. 2002. Mercury in bald eagle nestlings from South Carolina, USA. Journal of Wildlife Diseases 38:706-712.

Karstadt, M. L. 2007. Serum PFOA levels in residents of communities near a Teflon-production facility. Environmental Health Perspectives 115:A486–A487.

Kannon, K., J. Ridal, and J. Struger. 2006. Pesticides in the Great Lakes. Pages 151-199 *in* R. A. Hites editor. The handbook of environmental chemistry: Persistent organic pollutants in the Great Lakes. Springer-Verlag, Berlin and Heidelberg, Germany.

Kannon, K., L. Tao, E. Sinclair, S. D. Pastva, D. J. Jude, and J. Giesy. 2005. Perfluorinated compounds in aquatic organisms at various trophic levels in a Great Lakes food chain. Archives of Environmental Contamination and Toxicology 48:559-566.

Kannan, K., and J. Giesy. 2001. Global distribution of perfluorooctane sulfonate in wildlife. Environmental Science and Technology 35: 1339-1342.

Knobeloch L., M. Turyk, P. Imm, C. Schrank, and H. Anderson. 2008. Temporal changes in PCB and DDE levels among a cohort of frequent and infrequent consumers of Great Lakes sportfish. Environmental Research 109:66-72.

Kozie, K. D., and R. K. Anderson. 1991. Productivity, diet, and environmental contaminants in bald eagles nesting near the Wisconsin shoreline of Lake Superior. Archives of Environmental Contamination and Toxicology 20:41-48.

Kim, Y., M. Osako, and S. Sakai. 2006. Leaching characteristics of polybrominated diphenyl ethers (PBDEs) from flame-retardant plastics. Chemosphere 65:506-513.

Kramer, J. L., and P. T. Redig. 1997. Sixteen years of lead poisoning in eagles, 1980-95: An epizootiologic view. Journal of Raptor Research 31:327-332.

Kubwabo, C., N. Vais, and F. M. Benoit. 2004. A pilot study on the determination of perfluorooctanesulfonate and other perfluorinated compounds in blood of Canadians. Journal of Environmental Monitoring 6:540-545.

Lambertucci, S. A., J. A. Donzar, and F. Hiraldo. 2010. Poisoning people and wildlife with lead ammunition: Time to stop. Environmental Science and Technology 44:7759-7760.

Lee, K. E., and J. P. Anderson. 1998. Water-quality assessment of the upper Mississippi River basin, Minnesota and Wisconsin – polychlorinated biphenyls in common carp and walleye fillets, 1975-95. U. S. Geological Survey Water-Resources Investigations Report No. 98-4126.

Lewis, S. A., and R. W. Furness. 1991. Mercury accumulation and excretion in laboratory reared black-headed gull (*Larus ridibundus*) chicks. Archives of Environmental Contamination and Toxicology 21:316-320.

Magdalene S., D. R. Engstrom, and J. Elias. 2008. Large rivers water quality monitoring protocol, Version 1.0. National Park Service, Great Lakes Network, Ashland, Wisconsin. NPS/GLKN/NRR—2008/060. National Park Service, Fort Collins, Colorado.

Martin, P. A., D. Campbell, K. Hughes, and T. McDaniel. 2007. Lead in the tissues of terrestrial raptors in southern Ontario, Canada, 1995-2001. Science of the Total Environment 391:96-103.

Martin, J. W., D. C. G. Muir, C. A. Moody, D. A. Ellis, W. C. Kwan, K. R. Solomon, and S. A. Mabury. 2002. Collection of airborne fluorinated organics and analysis by gas chromatography/chemical ionization mass spectrometry. Analytical Chemistry 74: 584-590.

Martinez-Lopez, E., J. E. Martinez, P. Maria-Mojica, J. Penalver, M. Pulido, J. F. Calvo, and A. J. Garcia-Fernandez. 2004. Lead in feathers and δ- aminolevulinic acid dehydratase activity in three raptor species from an unpolluted Mediterranean forest (southern Spain). Archives of Environmental Contamination and Toxicology 47:270-275.

McKinney, M. A., L. S. Cesh, J. E. Elliott, T. D. Williams, D. K. Garcelon, and R. J. Letcher. 2006. Brominated flame retardants and halogenated phenolic compounds in North American west coast bald eaglet (*Haliaeetus leucocephalus*) plasma. Environmental Science and Technology 40:625-6281.

McPhail, J. D. 1997. A review of burbot (*Lota lota*) life-history and habitat use in relation to compensation and improvement opportunities. Canadian Manuscript Report of Fisheries and Aquatic Sciences 2397. Available at http://dsp-psd.pwgsc.gc.ca/collection_2007/dfo-mpo/Fs97-4-2397E.pdf (accessed 7 October 2010).

MDH (Minnesota Department of Health). 2005. Health consultation: Perfluorochemical releases at the 3M Cottage Grove facility. Available at http://www.atsdr.cdc.gov/HAC/pha/3M-CGF021805-MN/3M-CGF021805-MN_pt1.pdf (accessed 9 August 2010).

MDH. 2010. Public health assessment: Perflourochemical contamination in southern Washington County, northern Dakota County, and southeastern Ramsey County, Minnesota. Public comment release available at http://www.health.state.mn.us/div/eh/hazardous/index.html (accessed 31 August 2010).

Moody, C. A., J. W. Martin, W. C. Kwan, D. C. G. Muir, and S. A. Mabury. 2002. Monitoring perflourinated surfactants in biota and surface water samples following an accidental release of fire-fighting foam into Etobicoke Creek. Environmental Science and Technology 36: 545-551.

MPCA (Minnesota Pollution Control Agency). 2004. Estimated mercury emissions in Minnesota for 1990, 1995, and 2000. Minnesota Pollution Control Agency. Available at http://www.pca.state.mn.us/air/mercury.html (accessed 6 January 2009).

Monson, B. A. 2009. Trend reversal of mercury concentrations in piscivorous fish from Minnesota lakes: 1982—2006. Environmental Science and Technology 43:1750-1755.

Moraska-Lafrancois, B., and J. Glase. 2005. Aquatic studies in national parks of the upper Great Lakes states: Past efforts and future directions. U.S. Department of Interior, National Park Service report NPS/NRWRD/NRTR–2005/334. National Park Service, Denver, Colorado.

Nakayama, S. F., M. J. Strynar, J. L. Reiner, A. D. Delinsky, and A. B. Lindstrom. 2010. Determination of perfluorinated compounds in the upper Mississippi River basin. Environmental Science and Technology 44:4103-4109.

Newman, M. C., and M. A. Unger. 2003. Fundamentals of Ecotoxicology, 2nd edition. CRC Press, Boca Raton, Florida.

Newsted, J. L., P. D. Jones, K. Coady, and J. P. Giesy. 2005. Avian toxicity reference values for perfluorooctane sulfonate. Environmental Science and Technology 39:9357-9362.

Noble, D. G., and J. E. Elliot. 1990. Levels of contaminants in Canadian raptors, 1966 to 1988: Effects and temporal trends. Canadian Field-Naturalist 104:222-243.

Norstrom, R. J., M. Simon, J. Moisey, B. Wakeford, and D. V. C. Weseloh. 2002. Geographical distribution (2000) and temporal trends (1981-2000) of brominated diphenyl ethers in Great Lakes herring gull eggs. Environmental Science and Technology 36:4783-4789.

NLCD (National Land Cover Dataset). 2009. USGS product available at http://landcover.usgs.gov/natllandcover.php (accessed and downloaded in 2009).

Olsen, G. W., D. C. Mair, T. R. Church, M. E. Ellefson, W. K. Reagon, T. M. Boyd, R. M. Herron, Z. Medhdizadehkashi, J. B. Nobiletti, J. A. Rios, J. L. Butenhoff, and L. R. Zobel. 2008. Decline in perfluorooctanesulfonate and other polyfluoroalkyl chemicals in American Red Cross adult blood donors, 2000-2006. Environmental Science and Technology 42:4989-4995.

Ott, W. R. 1995. Environmental Statistics and Data Analysis. Lewis Publishers, Boca Raton, Florida.

Park, J., S. Oh, M. Shin, M. Kim, S. Yi, and K. Zoh. 2008. Seasonal variation in dissolved gaseous mercury and total mercury concentrations in Juam Reservoir, Korea. Environmental Pollution 154:12-20.

Pain, D., I. Fisher, and V. Thomas. 2008. A global update of lead poisoning in terrestrial birds from ammunition sources. Conference on Ingestion of Spent Lead Ammunition: Implications for Wildlife and Humans. Boise State University, Boise, ID. Available at: http://www.peregrinefund.org/Lead_conference (accessed 27 July 2010).

Pattee, O. H., and S. K. Hennes. 1983. Bald eagles and waterfowl: The lead shot connection. Transactions of the North American Wildlife and Natural Resource Conference 48:230-237.

Postupalsky, S. 1983. Techniques and terminology for surveys of nesting bald eagles. Appendix D *in* J. W. Grier, J. B. Elder, F. J. Gramlich, N. F. Green, J. V. Kussman, J. E. Mathisen, and J. P. Mattsson, editors. Northern states bald eagle recovery plan. U.S. Department of Interior, U.S. Fish and Wildlife Service, Twin Cities, Minnesota.

PRISM Climate Group. 2010. Data available at http://prism.nacse.org/ (accessed 31 March 2010).

Rapaport, R. A., and S. J. Eisenreich. 1988. Historical atmospheric inputs of high molecular weight chlorinated hydrocarbons to eastern North America. Environmental Science and Technology 22:931-941.

Rasmussen, P. W., C. S. Schrank, and P. A. Campfield. 2007. Temporal trends of mercury concentrations in Wisconsin walleye (*Sander vitreus*), 1982-2005. Ecotoxicology 116:541-550.

Renner, R. 2000. PBDE Polybrominated diphenyl ether. What fate for brominated fire retardants? Environmental Science and Technology 34:222-236.

Redig, P. T., D. R. Smith, and L. Cruz-Martinez. 2009. Potential sources of lead exposure for bald eagles: A retrospective study. Extended abstract *in* R. T. Watson, M. Fuller, M. Pokras, and W. G. Hunt, editors. Ingestion of lead from spent ammunition: Implications for wildlife and humans. The Peregrine Fund, Boise, Idaho.

Roberts, D. R., S. Manguin, and J. Mouchet. 2000. DDT house spraying and re-emerging malaria. Lancet 356:330-332.

Scheuhammer, A. M., and S. L. Norris. 1996. The ecotoxicology of lead shot and lead fishing weights. Ecotoxicology 5:279–295.

Scheuhammer, A. M., N. Basu, N. M. Burgess, J. E. Elliot, G. D. Campbell, M. Wayland, L. Champoux, and J. Rodrigue. 2008. Relationships among mercury, selenium, and neurochemical parameters in common loons (*Gavia immer*) and bald eagles (*Haliaeetus leucocephalus*). Ecotoxicology 17:93-101.

Scott, B. F., A. O. De Silva, C. Spencer, E. Lopez, S. M. Backus, and D. C. G. Muir. 2010. Perfluoroalkyl acids in Lake Superior water: Trends and sources. Journal of Great Lakes Research 36:277-284.

Searle, S. R. 1987. Linear Models for Unbalanced Data. Wiley, New York.

Simcik, M. F., and K. J. Dorweiler. 2005. Ratio of perfluorochemical concentrations as a tracer of atmospheric deposition to surface waters. Environmental Science and Technology 39:8678–8683.

Song, W., A. Li, J. C. Ford, N. C. Sturchio, K. J. Rockne, D. R. Buckley, and W. J. Mills. 2005. Polybrominated diphenyl ethers in the sediments of the Great Lakes. 2. Lakes Michigan and Huron. Environmental Science and Technology 39:3474-3479.

Sprunt, A., IV, W. B. Robertson, Jr., S. Postupalsky, R. J. Hensel, C. E. Knoder, and F. J. Ligas. 1973. Comparative productivity of six bald eagle populations. Transactions of North American Wildlife and Natural Resources Conference 38:96-106.

Stapleton, H. M., N. G. Dodder, J. H. Offenberg, M. M. Schantz, and S. A. Wise. 2004. Polybrominated diphenyl ethers in house dust and clothes dryer lint. Environmental Science and Technology 39:925-931.

Stickel, W. H., L. F. Stickel, R. A. Dyrland, and D. L. Hughes. 1984. DDE in birds: Lethal residues and loss rates. Archives of Environmental Contamination and Toxicology 13:1-6.

Strachan, W., and S. Eisenreich. 1988. Mass balancing of toxic chemicals in the Great Lakes: The role of atmospheric deposition. Appendix 1 of the Workshop of Great Lakes Atmospheric Deposition. International Joint Commission. Available at www.ijc.org/php/publications.

Stranberg, B., N. G. Dodder, I. Basu, and R. A. Hites. 2001. Concentrations and spatial variations of polybrominated diphenyl ethers and other organohalogen compounds in Great Lakes air. Environmental Science and Technology 35:1078-1083.

Talsness, C. E. 2008. Overview of toxicological aspects of polybrominated diphenyl ethers: A flame-retardant additive in several consumer products. Environmental Research 108:158-167.

Tomy, G. T., S. A. Tittlemier, V. P. Palace, W. R. Budakowski, E. Braekevelt, L. Brinkworth, and K. Friesen. 2004. Biotransformation of N-ethyl perfluorooctanesulfonamide by rainbow trout (*Onchorhynchus mykiss*) liver microsomes. Environmental Science and Technology 38:758-762.

U. S. Energy Information Administration. 2010. International energy outlook: 2010. Available at http://www.eia.doe.gov/oiaf/ieo/coal.html (accessed 9 August 2010).

USEPA (U.S. Environmental Protection Agency). 1995. Final water quality guidance for the Great Lakes. Federal Register 60:15366-15425.

USEPA. 2008. Toxic release inventory. U.S. Environmental Protection Agency Toxic Release Database available at http://www.epa.gov/triexplorer/statefactsheet.htm (accessed 9 August 2010).

USEPA. 2010. Monitoring report on environmental contaminants. Available at
http://www.epa.gov/glnpo/glindicators/fishtoxics/topfishb.html (accessed 9 August 2010).

USGS (U. S. Geological Survey). 2010. About the upper Mississippi River system. Available at
http://www.umesc.usgs.gov (accessed 16 June 2010).

Vonderheide, A. P., K. E. Mueller, J. Meija, and G. L. Welsh. 2008. Polybrominated diphenyl
ethers: Causes for concern and knowledge gaps regarding environmental distribution and
toxicity. Science of the Total Environment 400:425-436.

Wan, H., J. Perry, R. Ferrin, and B. Moraska-Lafrancois. 2007. Aquatic habitat classification on
the St. Croix National Scenic Riverway. Research report to the U.S. National Park Service.
University of Minnesota, St. Paul, Minnesota.

Welch, L. J. 1994. Contaminant burdens and reproductive rates of bald eagles breeding in Maine.
Thesis. University of Maine, Orono, Maine.

WHO (World Health Organization). 1994. International program on environmental safety;
environmental health criteria 162; brominated diphenyl ethers. Available at
http://www.inchem.org/documents/ehc/ehc/ehc162.htm (accessed 9 August 2010).

WICCI (Wisconsin Initiative on Climate Change Impacts). 2010. How is Wisconsin's climate
changing? Available at http://www.wicci.wisc.edu/ (accessed 23 July 2010).

Wiemeyer, S. N., T. J. Lamont, C. M. Bunck, C. R. Sindelar, F. J. Gramlich, J. D. Fraser, and M.
A. Byrd. 1984. Organochlorine pesticide, polychlorobiphenyl, and mercury residues in bald
eagle eggs – 1969-1979 – and their relationships to shell thinning and reproduction. Archives
of Environmental Contaminants and Toxicology 13:529-549.

Wiener, J. G., and M. B. Sandheinrich. 2010. Contaminants in the upper Mississippi River:
Historic trends, responses to regulatory controls, and emerging concerns. Hydrobiologia
640:49-70.

Wiener, J. G., D. P. Krabbenhoft, G. H. Heinz, and A. M. Scheuhammer. 2003. Ecotoxicology of
mercury. Pages 409-463 in D. J. Hoffman, B. A. Rattner, G. A. Burton, Jr., and J. Cairns, Jr.,
editors. Handbook of ecotoxicology, 2nd edition. CRC Press, Boca Raton, Florida.

Wood, P. B., J. H. White, A. Steffer, J. M. Wood, C. F. Facemire, and H. F. Percival. 1996.
Mercury concentrations in tissues of Florida bald eagles. Journal of Wildlife Management
60:178-185.

Ye, X., H. L. Schoenfuss, N. D. Jahns, A. D. Delinsky, M. J. Strynar, J. Varns, S. F. Nakayma,
L. Helfant, and A. B. Lindstrom. 2008a. Perfluorinated compounds in common carp
(Cyprinus carpio) fillets from the upper Mississippi River. Environment International
34:932-938.

Ye, X., M. J. Strynar, S. F. Nakayma, J. Varns, L. Helfant, J. Lazorchak, and A. B. Lindstrom. 2008*b*. Perfluorinated compounds in whole fish homogenates from the Ohio, Missouri, and upper Mississippi rivers, USA. Environmental Pollution 156:1227-1232.

Appendix A. PBDE, PFC, and PCB congeners analyzed in bald eagle plasma by the Wisconsin State Laboratory of Hygiene, 2006-2009.

Nine polybrominated diphenyl ethers (PBDEs):	Sixteen perfluorinated chemicals (PFCs):
PBDE #28	*Perflouro-N-tetradecanoic acid (PFTeDA)
PBDE #47	*Perflouro-N-tridecanoic acid (PFTrDA)
PBDE #66	*Perfluoro-1-butanesulfonate (PFBS)
PBDE #85	*Perfluoro-1-decanesulfonate (PFDS)
PBDE #99	*Perfluoro-1-heptanesulfonate (PFHpS)
PBDE #100	*Perfluoro-1-hexanesulfonate (PFHxS)
PBDE #138	Perfluoro-1-octanesulfonate (PFOS)
PBDE #153	*Perfluoro-N-butanoic acid (PFBA)
PBDE #154	*Perfluoro-N-decanoic acid (PFDA)
	*Perfluoro-N-dodecanoic acid (PFDoA)
	*Perfluoro-N-heptanoic acid (PFHpA)
	*Perfluoro-N-hexanoic acid (PFHxA)
	*Perfluoro-N-nonanoic acid (PFNA)
	Perfluoro-N-octanoic acid (PFOA)
	*Perfluoro-N-pentanoic acid (PFPA)
	*Perfluoro-N-undecanoic acid (PFuDA)

* = PFCs done in 2008 and 2009 only; PFOS and PFOA done all four years.

Seventy-five polychlorinated biphenyls (PCBs). Those separated by "/" could not be differentiated:

3	66	151	004/010	137/176
6	74	158	007/009	163/138
18	82	167	008/005	170/190
19	83	172	015/017	187/182
22	85	174	016/032	202/171
25	87	177	024/027	203/196
26	89	178	028/031	208/195
33	91	180	037/042	
40	95	183	041/071/064	
44	97	185	047/048	
45	99	193	056/060	
46	101	194	070/076	
49	118	198	077/110	
51	128	199	092/084	
52	136	201	123/149	
53	141	206	132/153/105	
63	146	207	135/144	

Appendix B. Quality assurance spikes conducted by the Wisconsin State Laboratory of Hygiene for contaminants in bald eagle plasma.

Quality Assurance Spikes – 2009 (From Wisconsin State Lab of Hygiene, 2009 eagle serum analytical laboratory report.)

Analyte	N	Average % Recovery	Standard Deviation
PCB #14 (3,5) - SURROGATE SPIKE	39	76.6	10.5
PCB #65 (2,3,5,6) - SURROGATE SPIKE	39	87.9	11.9
PCB #166 (2,3,4,4',5,6) - SURROGATE SPIKE	39	85.9	6.1
PCB #3	5	65.2	13.3
PCB #4/10	5	76	8.9
PCB #7/9	5	78.1	6.5
PCB #6	5	67.7	7.8
PCB #8/5	5	76.3	5.9
PCB #19	5	81.1	6.3
PCB #18	5	78.5	4.4
PCB #15/17	5	79.2	3.4
PCB #24/27	5	84.7	15.3
PCB #16/32	5	79.3	4.7
PCB #26	5	76.4	9.7
PCB #25	5	82	5.7
PCB #28/31	5	82.9	4.1
PCB #33	5	86.7	5.4
PCB #53	5	88.9	7
PCB #51	5	90.8	8.4
PCB #22	5	86.4	5.6
PCB #45	5	85.7	7.2
PCB #46	5	84.8	1.9
PCB #52	5	86.5	4.8
PCB #49	5	87.1	4.9
PCB #47/48	5	85.9	5.3
PCB #44	5	89.3	4.9
PCB #37/42	5	86	4.2
PCB #41/71/64	5	88.4	6.3
PCB #40	5	87.4	3.6
PCB #63	5	84.8	20.5
PCB #74	5	95	5.2
PCB #70/76	5	92.8	5.2
PCB #66	5	93.5	7.1
PCB #95	5	87.1	6
PCB #91	5	91.3	3.8
PCB #56/60	5	97	4.8
PCB #92/84	5	97.2	2.6
PCB #89	5	93.9	3.1
PCB #101	5	93.9	3.4

Analyte	N	Average % Recovery	Standard Deviation
PCB #99	5	90.8	3.9
PCB #83	5	97.3	4.4
PCB #97	5	94.6	4
PCB #87	5	94.2	4.6
PCB #85	5	98.7	3.6
PCB #136	5	94.3	6.4
PCB #77/110	5	94.3	6
PCB #82	5	88	2.8
PCB #151	5	90.8	3.4
PCB #135/144	5	88.1	1.9
PCB #123/149	5	89.6	2.4
PCB #118	5	88.8	1.2
PCB #146	5	87.2	1.5
PCB #132/153/105	5	86.7	1.2
PCB #141	5	92.3	0
PCB #137/176	5	87.3	2
PCB #163/138	5	88.8	1.8
PCB #158	5	100.9	2
PCB #178	5	87.7	1.2
PCB #187/182	5	90	3
PCB #183	5	92.9	0
PCB #128	5	90.6	1.7
PCB #167	5	90.2	1.7
PCB #185	5	90.8	2.4
PCB #174	5	89.2	1.7
PCB #177	5	88.6	3.9
PCB #202/171	5	85.5	5.8
PCB #172	5	85.4	2.2
PCB #180	5	91.9	1.6
PCB #193	5	92.2	2.3
PCB #199	5	94.1	2.1
PCB #170/190	5	90	3.4
PCB #198	5	96.3	2.6
PCB #201	5	93.1	3.3
PCB #203/196	5	93.5	3.1
PCB #208/195	5	93.4	3
PCB #207	5	94.1	2.9
PCB #194	5	91.8	3.2
PCB #206	5	93.8	3.5

Analyte	N	Average % Recovery	Standard Deviation
PBDE #28	5	100.2	11.4
PBDE #47	5	91.4	4.9
PBDE #66	5	98.6	6.5
PBDE #100	5	112	4.5
PBDE #99	5	96.8	8.4
PBDE #85	5	114	5.5
PBDE #154	5	118	8.4
PBDE #153	5	116	5.5
PBDE #138	5	126	5.5
P,P'-DDD	5	85	13.9
P,P'-DDT	5	96	15.2
p,p'-DDE	5	100.2	6.7
PFOS	8	92.4	13.9
PFOA	4	100	4.3
PFBS	4	88.8	3.8
PFHxS	4	93.5	4.4
PFHpS	4	90.3	5.1
PFDS	8	84.5	13.8
PFBA	4	155	70
PFPA	4	93	3.4
PFHxA	4	94.3	4.8
PFHpA	4	92.8	2.5
PFNA	4	102.5	7.5
PFDA	4	112.8	12.8
PFuDA	4	90.8	15.3
PFDoA	4	274.5	202.7
PFTrDA	4	113	24
PFTeDA	4	84	18

Appendix B. Quality assurance spikes conducted by the Wisconsin State Laboratory of Hygiene for contaminants in bald eagle plasma (continued).

Quality Assurance Spikes – 2008 (From Wisconsin State Lab of Hygiene, 2008 eagle serum analytical laboratory report.)

Analyte	N	Average % Recovery	Standard Deviation
PCB #14 (3,5) - SURROGATE SPIKE	47	75.8	12.7
PCB #65 (2,3,5,6) - SURROGATE SP KE	47	91.4	11.4
PCB #166 (2,3,4,4',5,6) - SURROGATE SPIKE	47	95.1	6.8
PCB #3	5	68.1	12.4
PCB #4/10	5	88.8	10.6
PCB #7/9	5	83.6	5
PCB #6	5	66.5	5.1
PCB #8/5	5	80.5	12
PCB #19	5	81	7.5
PCB #18	5	83.1	5.8
PCB #15/17	5	82.5	8.4
PCB #24/27	5	85.6	17.8
PCB #16/32	5	85	6.4
PCB #26	5	74	10.3
PCB #25	5	80	9.4
PCB #28/31	5	84	9.5
PCB #33	5	90	7.6
PCB #53	5	96.9	8
PCB #51	5	95.1	8.6
PCB #22	5	90	8.7
PCB #45	5	91.5	8.5
PCB #46	5	91.7	12.1
PCB #52	5	90.3	9.1
PCB #49	5	93.6	9
PCB #47/48	5	89.6	7.9
PCB #44	5	88	15.7
PCB #37/42	5	84.8	16.8
PCB #41/71/64	5	87.8	9
PCB #40	5	90	8
PCB #63	5	91.3	9.5
PCB #74	5	92.8	9.3
PCB #70/76	5	96.8	10.4
PCB #66	5	97.7	11.5
PCB #95	5	92.6	6.8
PCB #91	5	97.3	9.3
PCB #56/60	5	96.3	10.1
PCB #92/84	5	98.2	7.1
PCB #89	5	103.6	17.8
PCB #101	5	97.9	7.7

Analyte	N	Average % Recovery	Standard Deviation
PCB #99	5	94.8	7.2
PCB #83	5	101.5	10.5
PCB #97	5	95.8	12.8
PCB #87	5	99.7	8.2
PCB #85	5	100	11.4
PCB #136	5	101	8.4
PCB #77/110	5	91.9	15.4
PCB #82	5	93.6	5.4
PCB #151	5	95.7	4.7
PCB #135/144	5	96.4	4.1
PCB #123/149	5	96.5	3.6
PCB #118	5	96.7	5
PCB #146	5	95.6	4.2
PCB #132/153/105	5	94.5	7.2
PCB #141	5	99.1	6.8
PCB #137/176	5	94.6	3.8
PCB #163/138	5	96	4
PCB #158	5	105.5	5.9
PCB #178	5	90	5.4
PCB #187/182	5	97.1	6.4
PCB #183	5	98	5
PCB #128	5	96.6	3.8
PCB #167	5	95.6	4
PCB #185	5	97.9	4.5
PCB #174	5	96.2	5.4
PCB #177	5	93.1	5.6
PCB #202/171	5	93.5	2.8
PCB #172	5	100.5	12.9
PCB #180	5	98.1	3.6
PCB #193	5	99.4	6
PCB #199	5	95.9	1.6
PCB #170/190	5	87.8	17.1
PCB #198	5	99.2	3.5
PCB #201	5	94.3	8.1
PCB #203/196	5	94	13.7
PCB #208/195	5	93.4	11.1
PCB #207	5	86.4	28.1
PCB #194	5	91.1	12
PCB #206	5	95.9	6.5

Analyte	N	Average % Recovery	Standard Deviation
PBDE #28	5	101.6	10.5
PBDE #47	5	87.8	6.6
PBDE #66	5	94	8.3
PBDE #100	5	97.8	4.3
PBDE #99	5	90	7.3
PBDE #85	5	87.8	19.5
PBDE #154	5	91.8	8.5
PBDE #153	5	95.2	4.4
PBDE #138	5	95.4	16.8
P,P'-DDD	5	99.5	5.8
P,P'-DDT	5	81.1	13
p,p'-DDE	5	100.8	10.9
PFOS	32	103.8	7.7
PFOA	13	105.5	10.2
PFBS	13	105.9	8
PFHxS	13	96.6	23.2
PFHpS	13	96	11.8
PFDS	13	97.4	25.1
PFBA	13	91.9	18.3
PFPA	13	93.1	29.6
PFHxA	13	95.7	15.6
PFHpA	13	100	15
PFNA	13	107.1	13.9
PFDA	13	83.6	18.6
PFUdA	13	98.2	18
PFDoA	13	126.5	32.7
PFTrDA	13	86.6	18.5
PFTeDA	13	88.9	17.5

Appendix B. Quality assurance spikes conducted by the Wisconsin State Laboratory of Hygiene for contaminants in bald eagle plasma (continued).

Quality Assurance Spikes – 2007 (From Wisconsin State Lab of Hygiene, 2007 Eagle Serum Analytical Laboratory Report.)

Analyte	N	Average % Recovery	Standard Deviation	Analyte	N	Average % Recovery	Standard Deviation	Analyte	N	Average % Recovery	Standard Deviation
PCB #14 (3,5) - SURROGATE SPIKE	35	77.3	5.6	PCB #99	4	97.4	6.3	PBDE #28	4	96.8	9
PCB #65 (2,3,5,6) - SURROGATE SP KE	35	95.3	6.7	PCB #83	4	111	9.8	PBDE #47	4	97	3.9
PCB #166 (2,3,4,4',5,6) - SURROGATE SPIKE	35	103	15.4	PCB #97	4	103	6.6	PBDE #66	4	103	3.9
PCB #3	4	31	14.6	PCB #87	4	106	1.9	PBDE #100	4	111	4
PCB #4/10	4	65.3	16.2	PCB #85	4	104	17.1	PBDE #99	4	100	7.1
PCB #7/9	4	70.4	4.3	PCB #136	4	102	10.7	PBDE #85	4	112	5.5
PCB #6	4	73.2	3.5	PCB #77/110	4	107	3.7	PBDE #154	4	113	7.1
PCB #8/5	4	77.9	3.9	PCB #82	4	88.7	3.4	PBDE #153	4	115	10.9
PCB #19	4	80.5	3.7	PCB #151	4	90.1	3.1	PBDE #138	4	126	16.2
PCB #18	4	81.2	5	PCB #135/144	4	90.5	3.2				
PCB #15/17	4	77.2	8.7	PCB #123/149	4	92.9	5.9	P,P'-DDD	4	114	19.5
PCB #24/27	4	85.5	6.5	PCB #118	4	95.7	7.6	P,P'-DDT	4	103	8.7
PCB #16/32	4	87.3	5.1	PCB #146	4	89.3	3.6	p,p'-DDE	4	102	2.6
PCB #26	4	67.7	6.1	PCB #132/153/105	4	88.7	5.9				
PCB #25	4	74.6	2.1	PCB #141	4	89.9	6.5				
PCB #28/31	4	84.7	5	PCB #137/176	4	92.4	6.3				
PCB #33	4	85.7	6.2	PCB #163/138	4	93.6	5.1				
PCB #53	4	99.8	5.7	PCB #158	4	110	15.8				
PCB #51	4	94.3	7.8	PCB #178	4	87.7	9.5				
PCB #22	4	96.2	10	PCB #187/182	4	92.5	5.7				
PCB #45	4	90.4	4.8	PCB #183	4	95.3	2.8				
PCB #46	4	92.2	6.3	PCB #128	4	94.9	1.2				
PCB #52	4	95.9	4.9	PCB #167	4	102	10.1				
PCB #49	4	94.9	4.6	PCB #185	4	96.5	4.4				
PCB #47/48	4	94.1	4.7	PCB #174	4	95.3	3.2				
PCB #44	4	94.3	0.7	PCB #177	4	94.1	2.3				
PCB #37/42	4	92.4	6.9	PCB #202/171	4	92	8.7				
PCB #41/71/64	4	93.4	5.3	PCB #172	4	99.9	6				
PCB #40	4	96.4	6.1	PCB #180	4	94.6	1.9				
PCB #63	4	90.6	15.1	PCB #193	4	108	14.6				
PCB #74	4	98.5	2.2	PCB #199	4	96.3	2.5				
PCB #70/76	4	103	5.9	PCB #170/190	4	91.9	2.8				
PCB #66	4	108	11.6	PCB #198	4	96.5	5.3				
PCB #95	4	95.2	7	PCB #201	4	94.3	5.1				
PCB #91	4	103	16	PCB #203/196	4	95.6	3.3				
PCB #56/60	4	103	3.5	PCB #208/195	4	96.5	2.9				
PCB #92/84	4	104	7.3	PCB #207	4	95.7	4				
PCB #89	4	106	15	PCB #194	4	95.8	10.3				
PCB #101	4	104	5.3	PCB #206	4	97.8	6.1				

Appendix B. Quality assurance spikes conducted by the Wisconsin State Laboratory of Hygiene for contaminants in bald eagle plasma (continued).

Quality Assurance Spikes – 2006 (From data files provided by the Wisconsin State Lab of Hygiene regarding the QA spikes for 2006.)

Analyte	N	Average % Recovery	Standard Deviation
PCB #14 (3,5) - SURROGATE SPIKE	32	83.5	10.5
PCB #65 (2,3,5,6) - SURROGATE SP KE	32	92.1	7.6
PCB #166 (2,3,4,4',5,6) - SURROGATE SPIKE	25	103.9	5.5
PCB #3	4	51.2	17.2
PCB #4/10	4	77.5	5.0
PCB #7/9	4	74.0	6.5
PCB #6	4	77.4	4.0
PCB #8/5	4	79.0	4.0
PCB #19	4	86.1	5.5
PCB #18	4	82.8	6.0
PCB #15/17	4	82.8	6.0
PCB #24/27	4	92.4	8.1
PCB #16/32	4	88.2	4.8
PCB #26	4	81.5	5.5
PCB #25	4	91.7	6.8
PCB #28/31	4	87.0	5.2
PCB #33	4	91.7	3.3
PCB #53	4	82.8	4.9
PCB #51	4	95.2	8.8
PCB #22	4	96.2	4.4
PCB #45	4	90.8	3.4
PCB #46	4	95.6	2.9
PCB #52	4	94.7	4.3
PCB #49	4	96.3	2.5
PCB #47/48	4	97.0	2.9
PCB #44	4	90.8	2.6
PCB #37/42	4	97.9	4.2
PCB #41/71/64	4	94.7	4.3
PCB #40	4	99.4	3.1
PCB #63	4	100.8	1.5
PCB #74	4	97.7	4.5
PCB #70/76	4	96.9	3.6
PCB #66	4	102.7	5.4
PCB #95	4	95.7	6.5
PCB #91	4	101.4	2.8
PCB #56/60	4	98.6	1.1
PCB #92/84	4	103.8	4.1
PCB #89	4	124.3	17.8
PCB #101	4	101.2	5.4

Analyte	N	Average % Recovery	Standard Deviation
PCB #99	4	100.0	2.6
PCB #83	4	99.5	8.8
PCB #97	4	100.0	5.5
PCB #87	4	102.0	6.0
PCB #85	4	106.0	7.6
PCB #136	4	97.0	13.0
PCB #77/110	4	101.7	4.9
PCB #82	4	96.9	3.6
PCB #151	4	95.3	0.9
PCB #135/144	4	99.5	3.1
PCB #123/149	4	98.3	3.3
PCB #118	4	106.9	7.4
PCB #146	4	98.9	2.2
PCB #132/153/105	4	96.1	0.9
PCB #141	4	96.8	1.1
PCB #137/176	4	105.8	3.8
PCB #163/138	4	100.8	3.9
PCB #158	4	103.5	14.6
PCB #178	4	99.5	2.3
PCB #187/182	4	98.6	2.8
PCB #183	4	99.7	2.2
PCB #128	4	98.2	1.4
PCB #167	4	105.8	6.7
PCB #185	4	100.0	3.4
PCB #174	4	95.6	2.9
PCB #177	4	97.8	1.8
PCB #202/171	4	100.0	1.9
PCB #172	4	108.1	8.5
PCB #180	4	100.0	0.0
PCB #193	4	103.3	4.2
PCB #199	4	97.8	2.5
PCB #170/190	4	93.2	4.5
PCB #198	4	97.8	5.8
PCB #201	4	101.1	2.2
PCB #203/196	4	100.0	0.0
PCB #208/195	4	99.5	1.1
PCB #207	4	92.7	11.8
PCB #194	4	100.0	0.0
PCB #206	4	101.6	1.1

Analyte	N	Average % Recovery	Standard Deviation
PBDE #28	4	101.1	9.1
PBDE #47	4	92.2	4.9
PBDE #66	4	89.8	2.1
PBDE #100	4	98.1	2.6
PBDE #99	4	97.2	6.9
PBDE #85	4	99.2	2.1
PBDE #154	4	100.0	6.3
PBDE #153	4	97.9	7.3
PBDE #138	4	103.6	4.1
P,P'-DDD	4	94.4	7.4
P,P'-DDT	4	115.0	9.8
p,p'-DDE	4	90.2	3.0

Appendix C. Limits of detection (LOD) or report limit (RL) and the percent of samples that were above them as reported by the Wisconsin State Laboratory of Hygiene for bald eagle plasma and feather samples tested for environmental contaminants, 2006-2009.

Table C-1. Limits of detection (LOD) or report limit (RL) and the percent of samples that were above and below them for six targeted contaminants that did not have multiple congeners.

Contaminant	LOD/RL	% ≥LOD	% ≤LOD
DDE	0.15	100.0	0.0
Mercury	0.004	100.0	0.0
Selenium	0.28	97.4	2.6
Lead	0.14	75.5	24.5
DDD	0.3	74.3	25.7
DDT	0.35	5.9	94.1

Table C-2. Percent of bald eagle plasma samples above the laboratories limits of detection (LOD) for 16 PFC and 9 PBDE congeners.

PFC telomer	% above LOD	PBDE congener	% above LOD
PFDS	100.0	47	100.0
PFDoA	100.0	99	94.7
PFHpS	100.0	100	94.1
PFHxS	100.0	153	88.8
PFNA	100.0	154	86.8
PFOS	100.0	28	43.4
PFTrDA	100.0	66	34.2
PFuDA	100.0	138	1.3
PFTeDA	98.8	85	0.0
PFDA	96.5		
PFOA	94.7		
PFBA	81.2		
PFHpA	20.0		
PFHxA	3.5		
PFPA	2.4		
PFBS	0.0		

Appendix C. Limits of detection (LOD) or report limit (RL) and the percent of samples that were above them as reported by the Wisconsin State Laboratory of Hygiene for bald eagle plasma and feather samples tested for environmental contaminants, 2006-2009 (continued).

Table C-3. List of PCB congeners in bald eagle plasma that were above the laboratory limits of detection (LOD; shown in parentheses) grouped by percent-categories. For example, the 15 congeners listed in the first column were detected at levels above the LOD >90% of the time. In all, 75 PCB congeners or congener pairings were considered; congener pairings separated by a slash could not be differentiated.

90% to 100%	80% to 90%	60% to 80%	40% to 60%	0% to 40%	Never
15 congeners:	*22 congeners:*	*9 congeners:*	*4 congeners:*	*18 congeners:*	*7 congeners:*
132/153/105 (0.15)	101 (0.1)	056/060 (0.1)	083 (0.1)	026 (0.15)	003 (6.0)
163/138 (0.15)	174 (0.07)	049 (0.1)	092/084 (0.15)	051 (0.1)	004/010 (0.7)
180 (0.1)	087 (0.1)	097 (0.1)	136 (0.2)	016/032 (0.2)	006 (0.2)
187/182 (0.07)	177 (0.07)	091 (0.15)	141 (0.1)	018 (0.15)	007/009 (0.15)
201 (0.1)	178 (0.1)	028/031 (0.3)		033 (0.15)	019 (0.15)
118 (0.15)	206 (0.07)	037/042 (0.1)		063 (0.1)	024/027 (0.15)
077/110 (0.1)	066 (0.15)	041/071/064 (0.15)		015/017 (0.2)	025 (0.15)
183 (0.07)	085 (0.1)	185 (0.07)		022 (0.2)	
170/190 (0.1)	095 (0.1)	082 (0.1)		045 (0.1)	
146 (0.1)	158 (0.15)			207 (0.07)	
123/149 (0.1)	167 (0.1)			053 (0.2)	
203/196 (0.15)	172 (0.1)			040 (0.1)	
128 (0.07)	151 (0.1)			046 (0.1)	
194 (0.07)	193 (0.1)			199 (0.07)	
099 (0.1)	208/195 (0.1)			198 (0.1)	
	135/144 (0.1)			089 (0.1)	
	052 (0.1)			008/005 (0.4)	
	070/076 (0.1)			137/176 (0.1)	
	202/171 (0.07)				
	074 (0.1)				
	044 (0.1)				
	047/048 (0.1)				

Appendix D. Spatial distribution of environmental contaminants monitored by the National Park Service, Great Lakes Inventory and Monitoring Network, at six study areas in the upper Midwest, 2006-2009.

The following spatial distribution maps summarize all data we collected on the contaminants we monitored. Samples that were below the laboratory limits of detection (LOD) were given zero and are shown as none-detects (white dots). Yearly summary maps show all data points for that year; no hidden values. Locations are generally within 100 m of the true location of each nest, depending on method of obtaining the location (aerial or from the ground) and on GPS accuracy.

Summary maps with maximum values provide the greatest concentration measured for that contaminant at each nest over the four years, hence all nests sampled over the four years show up exactly once and small values are hidden. The maximum value provides an assessment of exceedences and maximum levels. Compare yearly maps to examine annual variability.

Study areas were not sampled every year. The monitoring design called for sampling the three National Park Service areas in 2006 and 2007 and then on two-year rotations thereafter. Additional sample years and sampling in adjacent areas were added as partnerships and funding made it possible. Accordingly, Apostle Islands was not sampled in 2009; the Lake Superior South Shore was not sampled in 2006 or 2009; the upper St. Croix Riverway was not sampled in 2008 and 2009; and the Pools 3 & 4 study area was not sampled in 2006 and 2007.

Maps are shown in the order presented in the results section of the report.

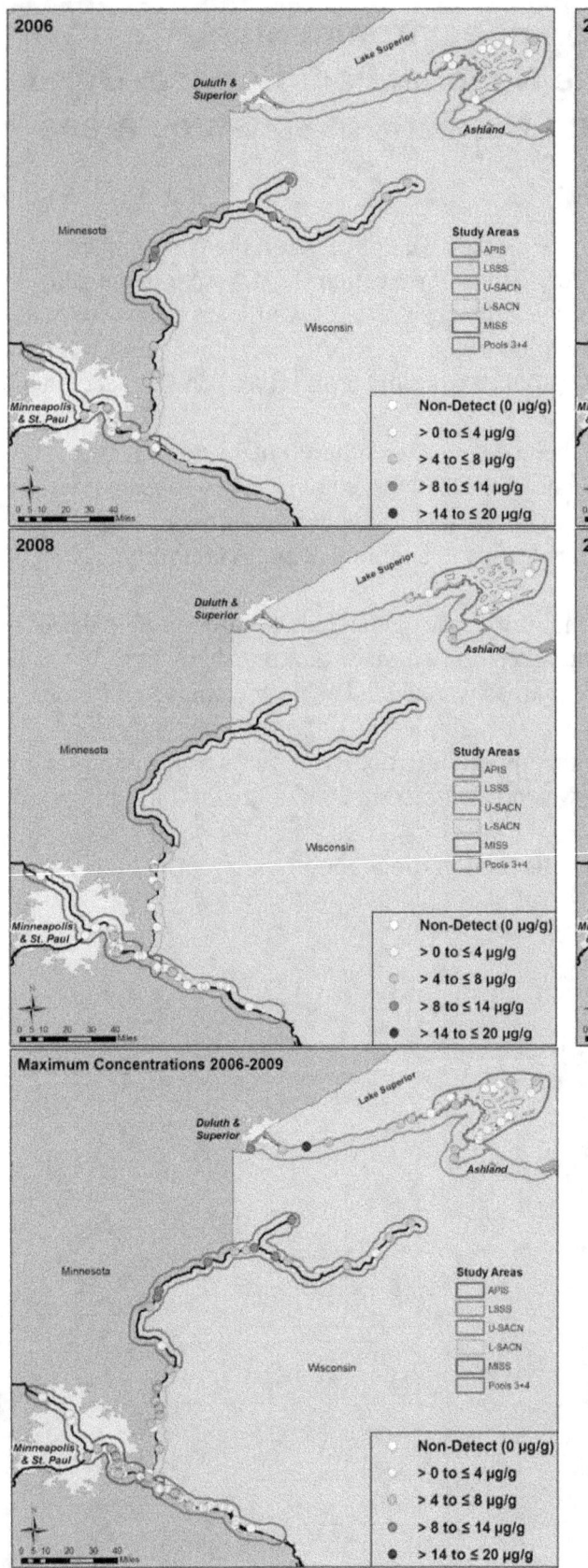

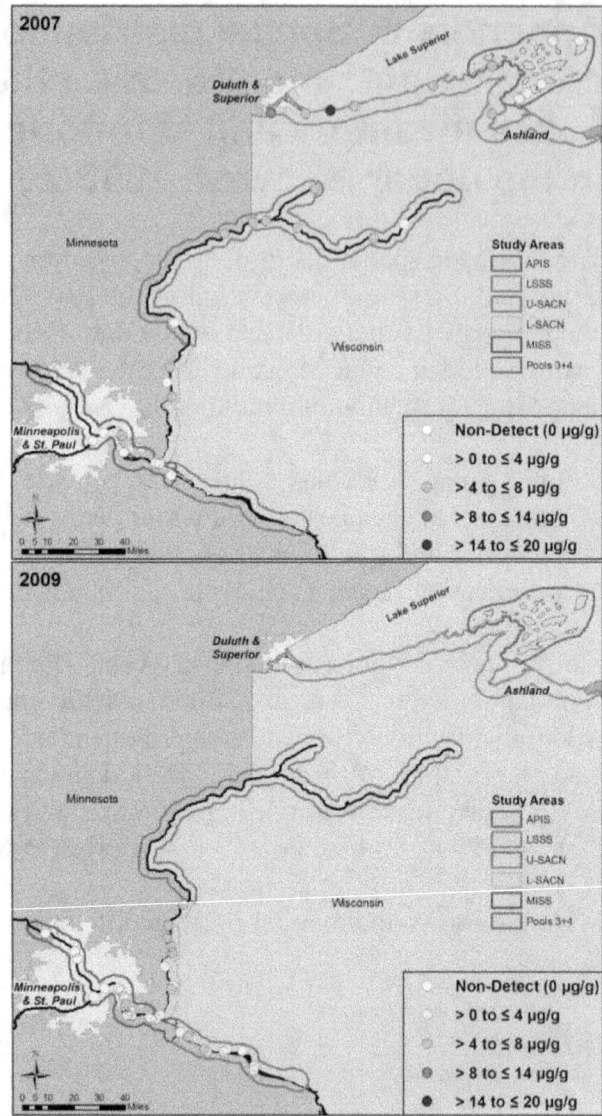

Figure D-1. Spatial distribution of *total mercury* measured in breast feathers of bald eagle nestlings sampled at their nest from six study areas in the upper Midwest, 2006-2009. Most of this mercury (>95%) is assumed to be methylmercury. We selected 7.5 *u*g/g (wet weight) of mercury in breast feathers as a provisional threshold above which toxicity may be indicated for some wildlife and humans. Nest locations shown as bright and dark red dots (first category rounded up from 7.5 to 8.0 *u*g/g) are above this provisional threshold.

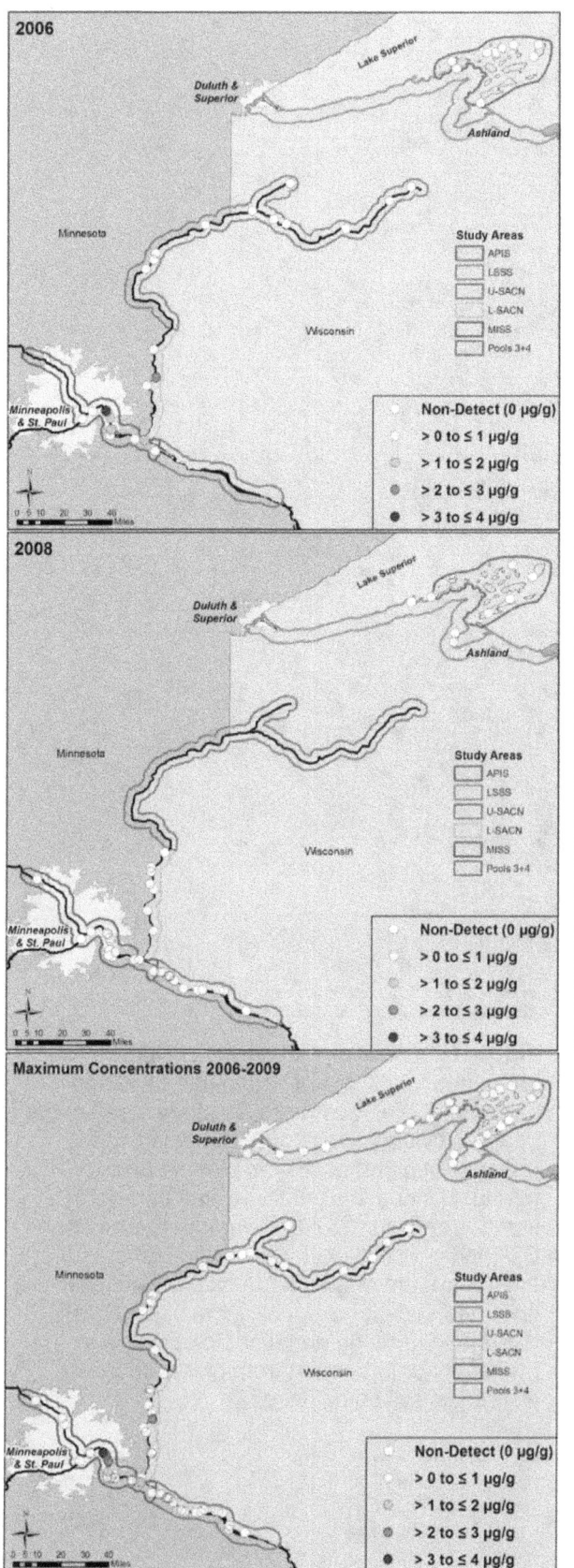

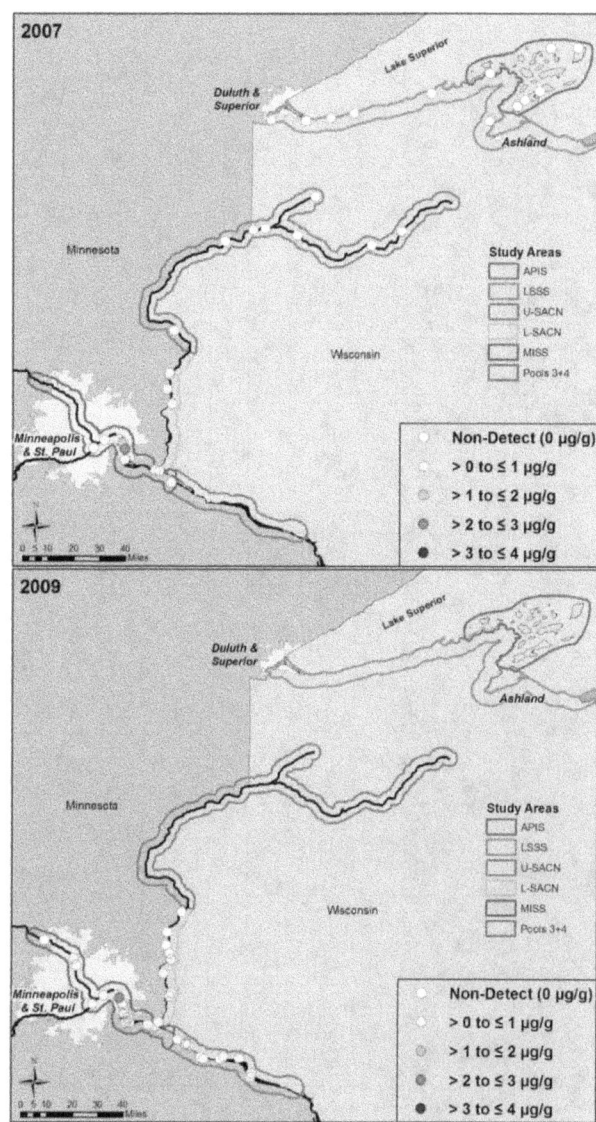

Figure D-2. Spatial distribution of *lead* measured in breast feathers of bald eagle nestlings sampled at their nest from six study areas in the upper Midwest, 2006-2009. We selected 2.0 *u*g/g (wet weight) of lead in breast feathers as a provisional threshold above which toxicity may be indicated for some wildlife and humans. Nest locations shown as bright and dark red dots are above this provisional threshold.

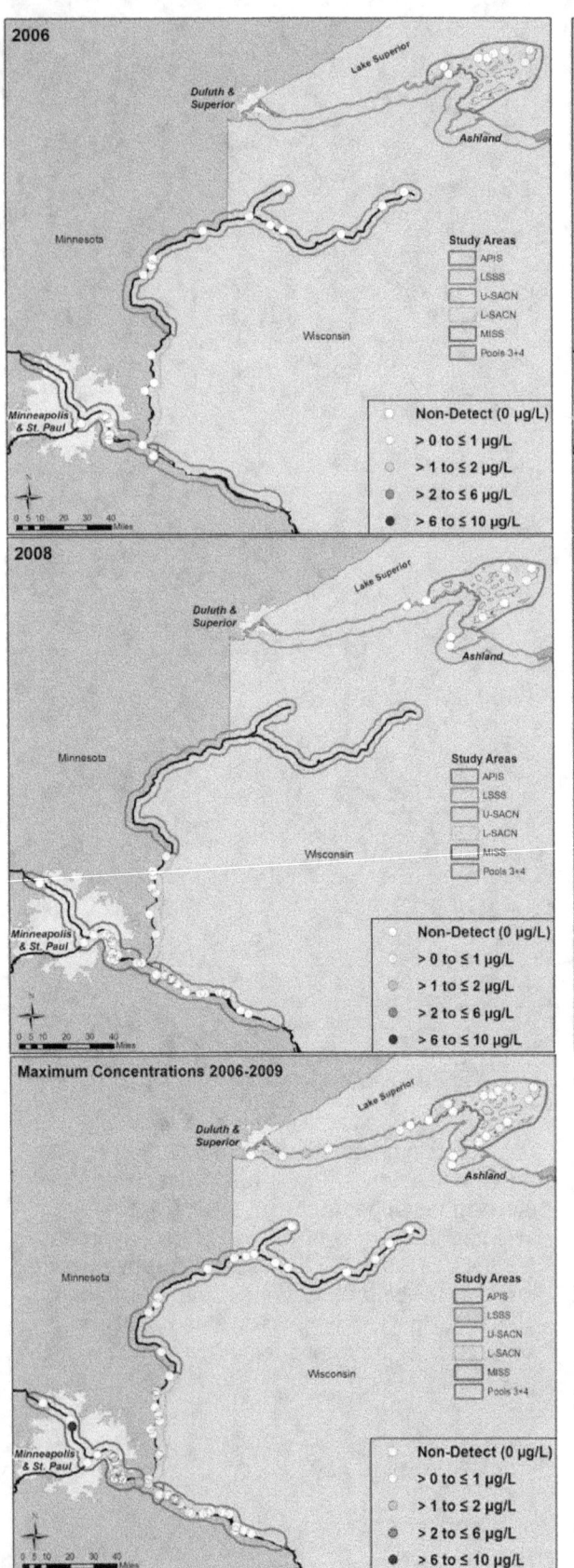

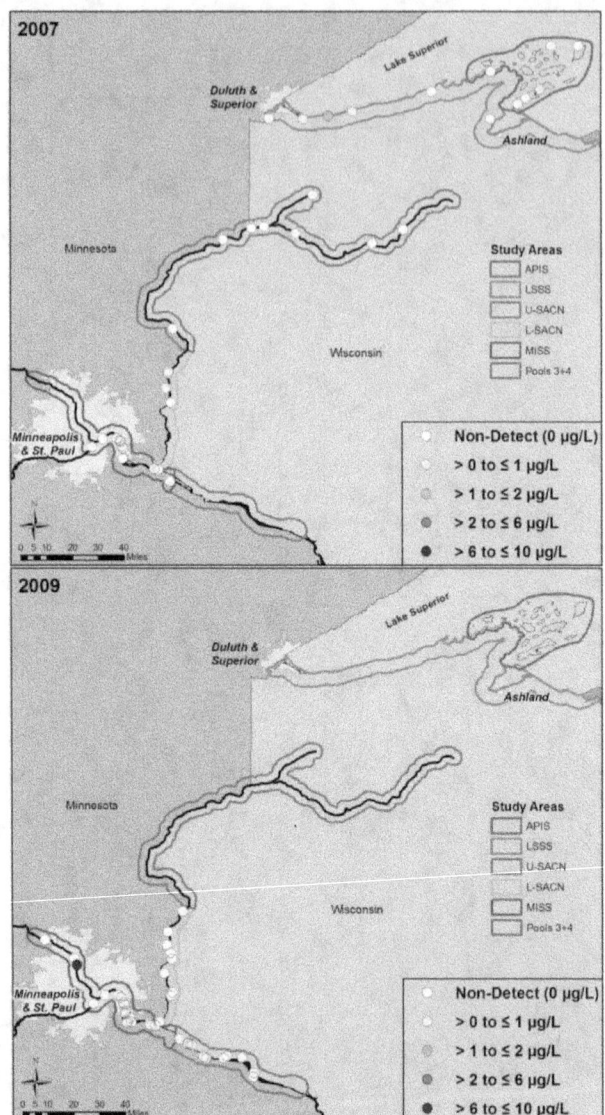

Figure D-3. Spatial distribution of ***DDT*** measured in plasma of bald eagle nestlings sampled at their nest from six study areas in the upper Midwest, 2006-2009. We selected 0.0 *u*g/L (wet weight) of DDT in plasma as our threshold since this pesticide was banned in North America in 1972. Several detections of DDT indicate this chemical continues to enter the ecosystem due either to its persistence in soils and sediments, local illegal use, and/or through long range aerial or biological (e.g. migrant birds) transport from global sources where it is still being used.

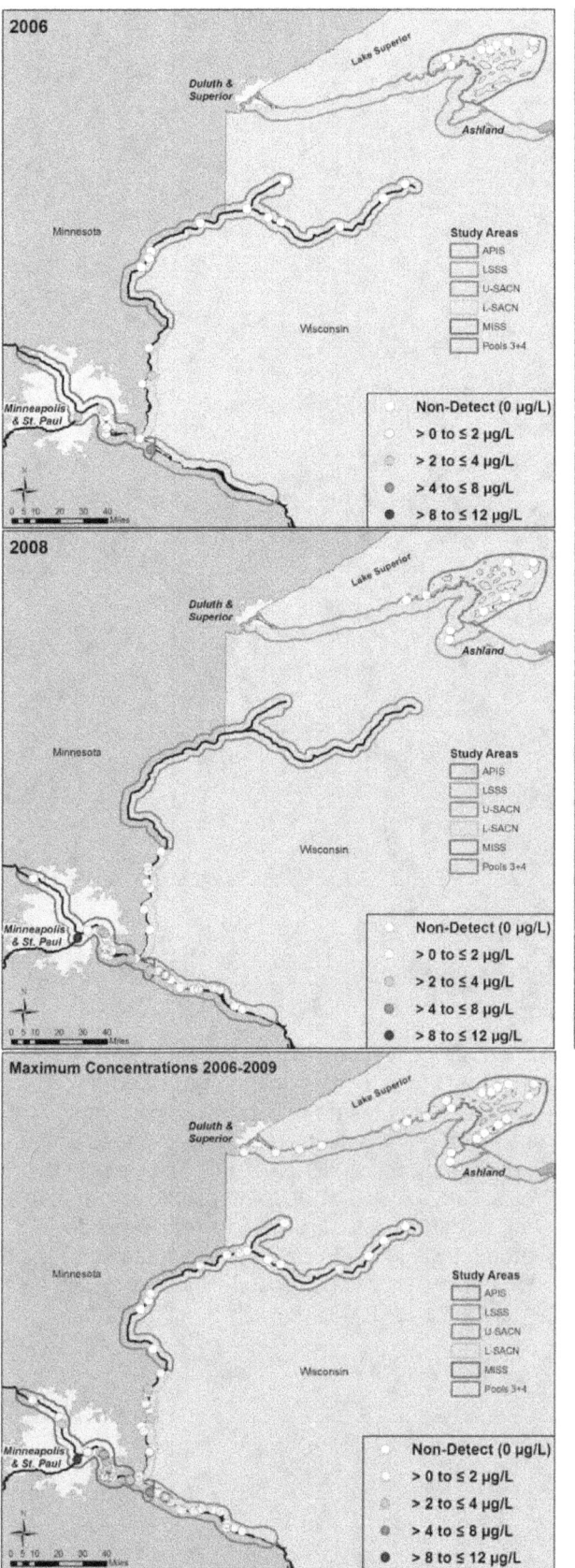

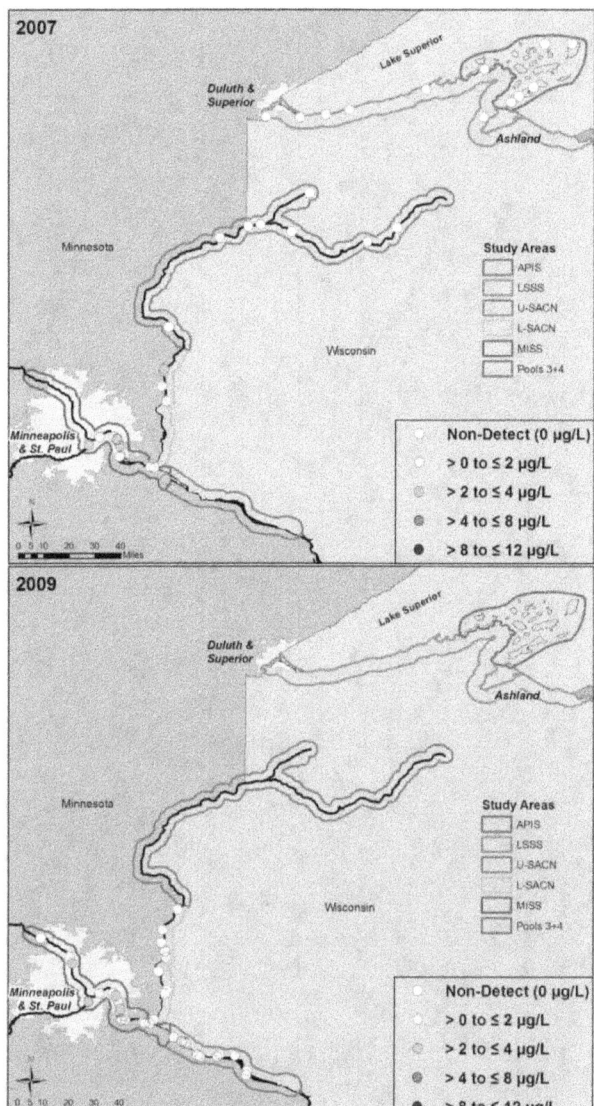

Figure D-4. Spatial distribution of **DDD** measured in plasma of bald eagle nestlings sampled at their nest from six study areas in the upper Midwest, 2006-2009. No threshold value has been determined. DDD is a metabolite of DDT.

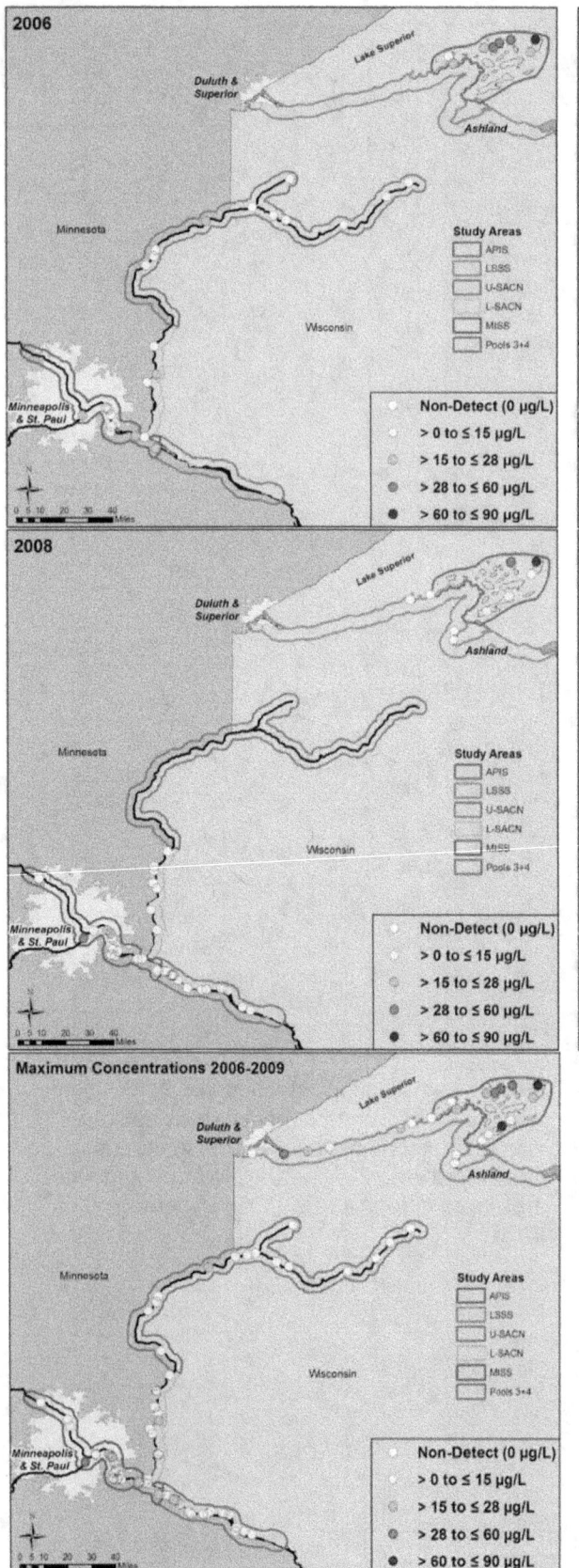

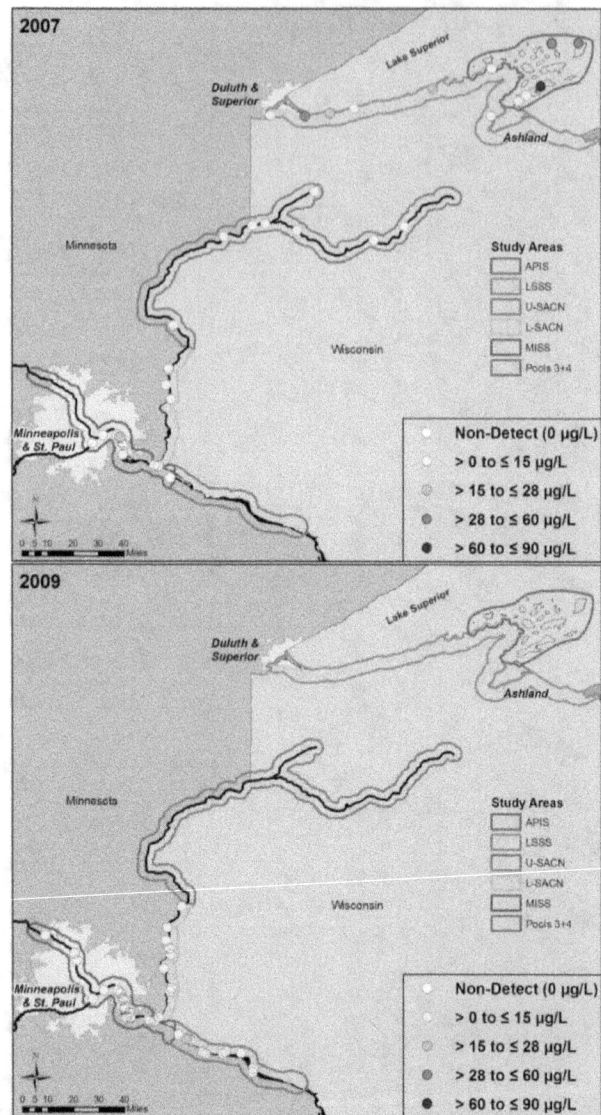

Figure D-5. Spatial distribution of *DDE* measured in plasma of bald eagle nestlings sampled at their nest from six study areas in the upper Midwest, 2006-2009. We selected 28.0 *u*g/L (wet weight) of DDE in nestling plasma as our threshold. Studies have linked lowered productivity in some bald eagle populations when concentrations reach this level. DDE is a metabolite of DDT.

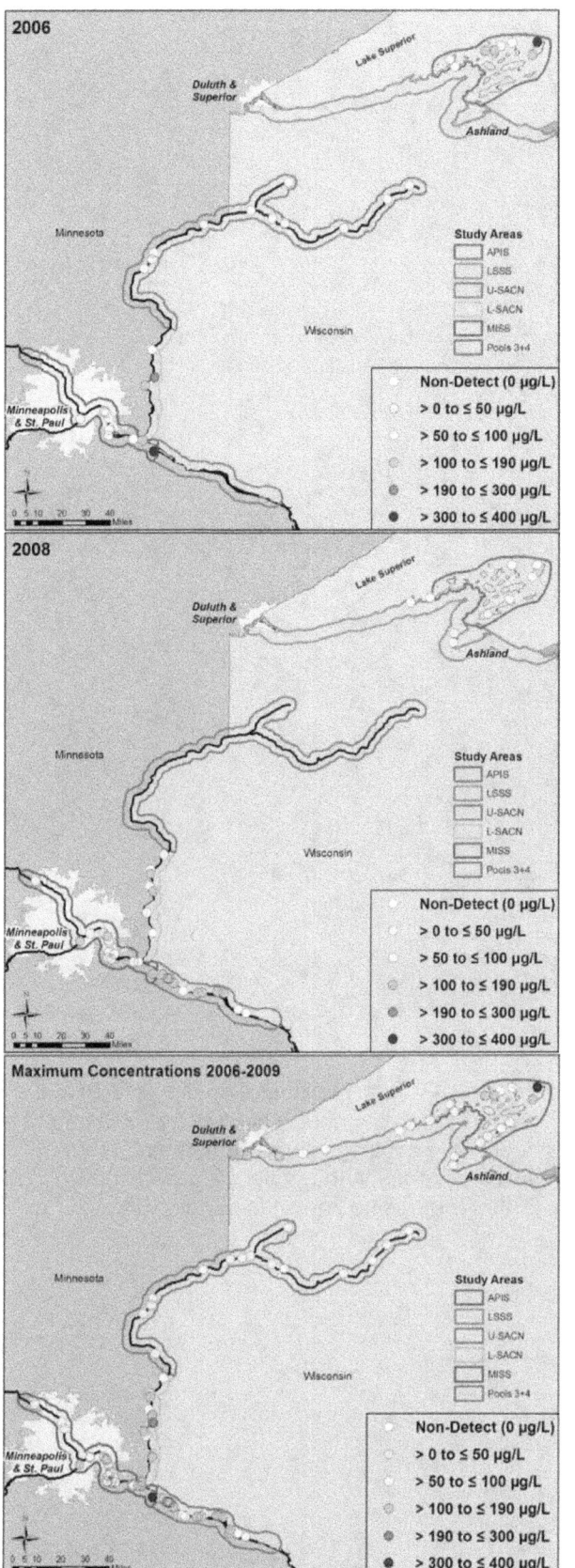

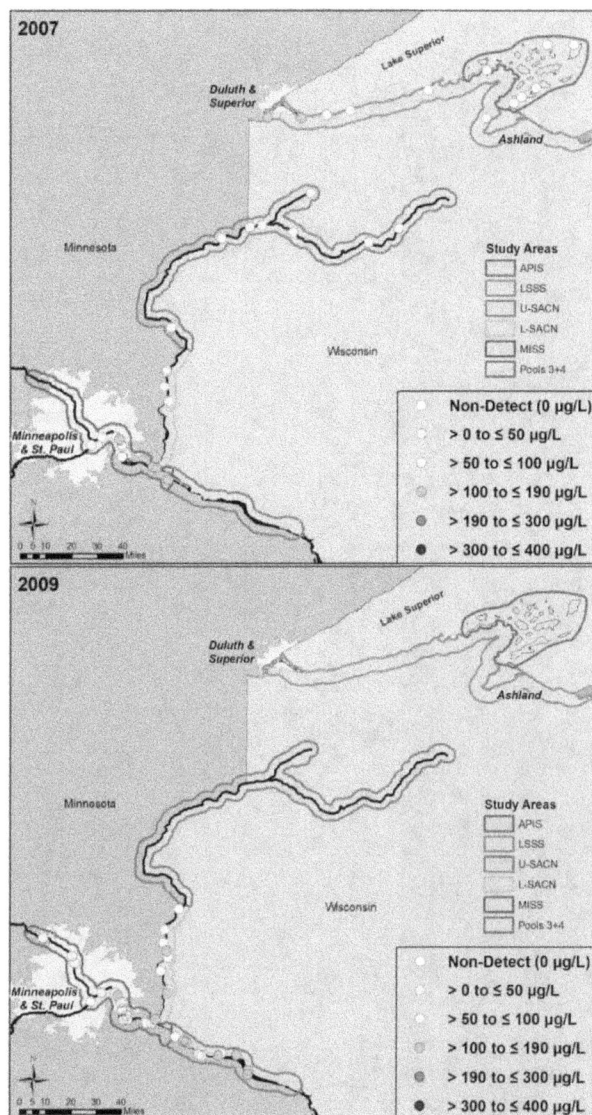

Figure D-6. Spatial distribution of total *PCBs* measured in plasma of bald eagle nestlings sampled at their nest from six study areas in the upper Midwest, 2006-2009. We selected 190.0 *u*g/L (wet weight) of PCBs in plasma as a threshold. Studies have linked reduced bald eagle reproductive rates when concentrations are above this level.

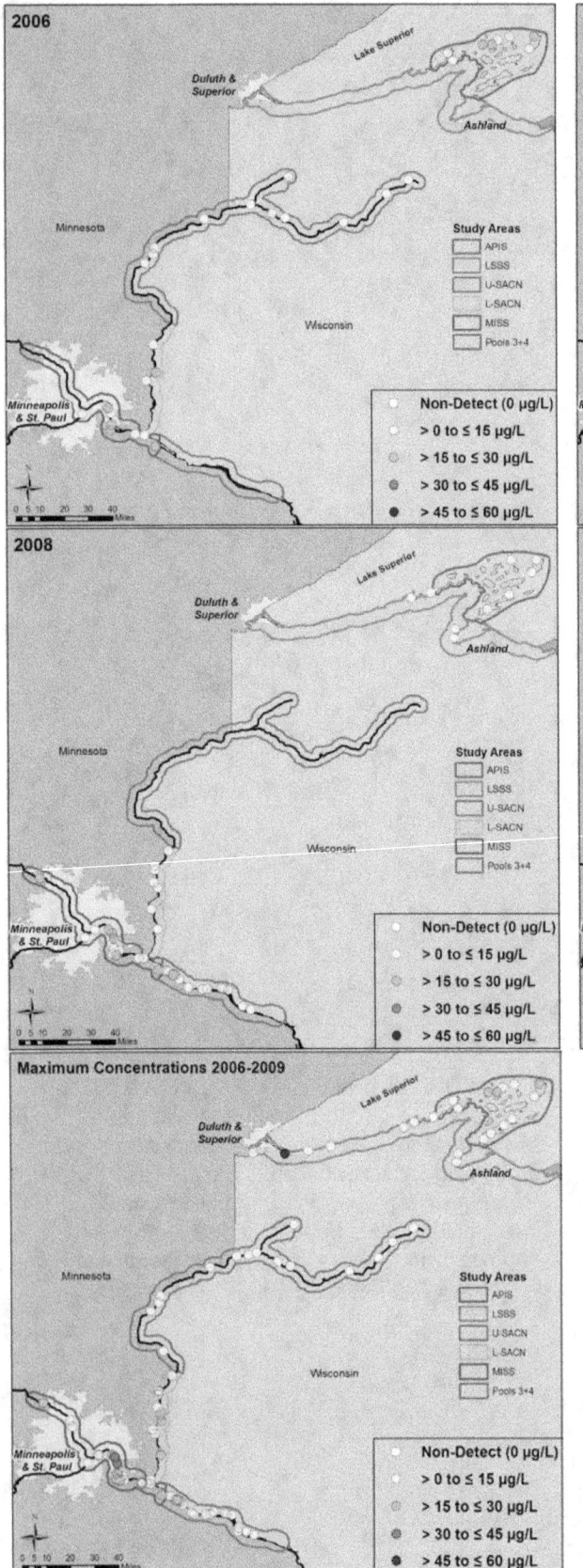

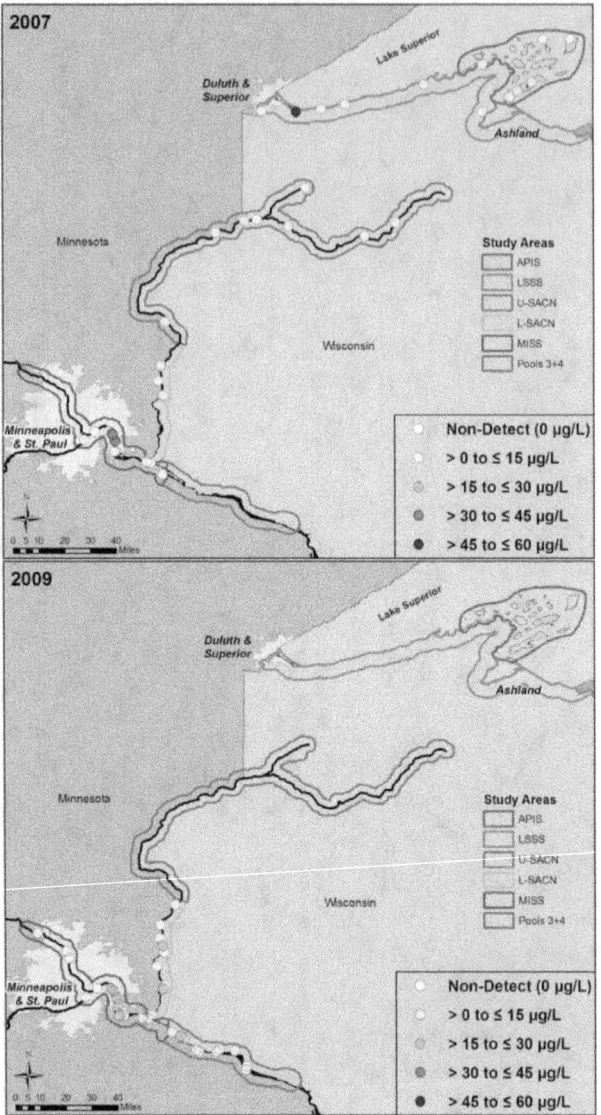

Figure D-7. Spatial distribution of total *PBDEs* (sum of nine congeners) measured in plasma of bald eagle nestlings sampled at their nest from six study areas in the upper Midwest, 2006-2009. There is no known threshold value.

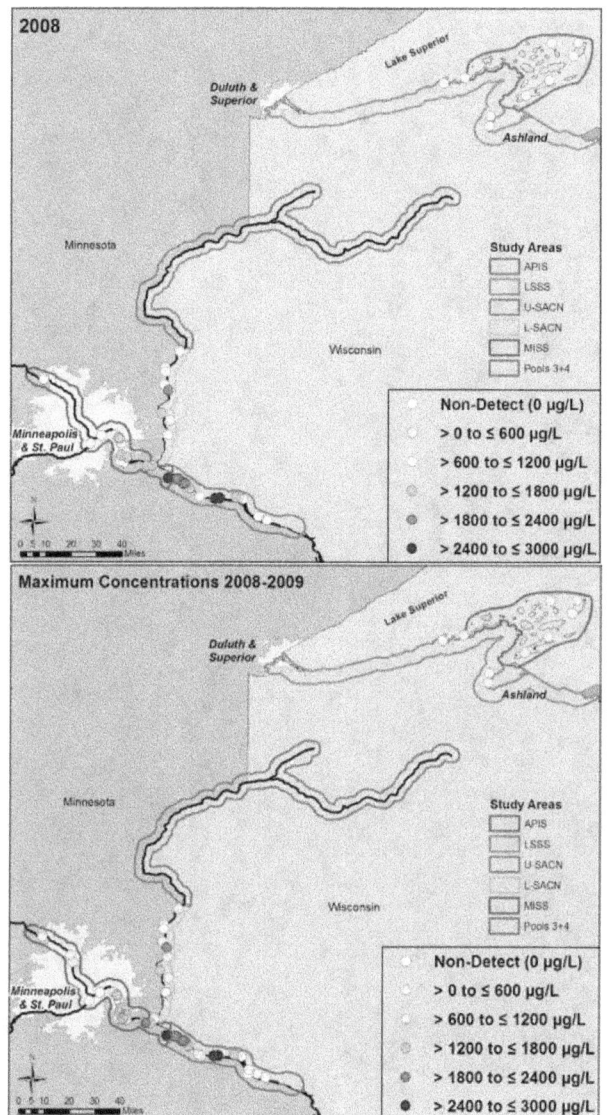

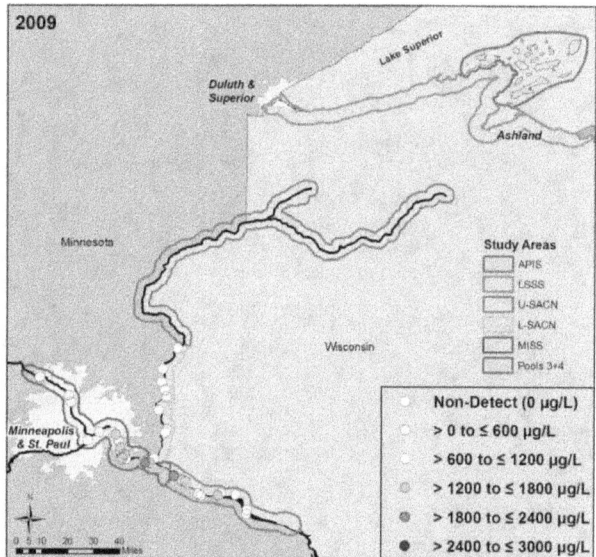

Figure D-8. Spatial distribution of total *PFCs* (sum of 16 congeners) measured in plasma of bald eagle nestlings sampled at their nest from six study areas in the upper Midwest, 2008 and 2009. There is no known threshold value.

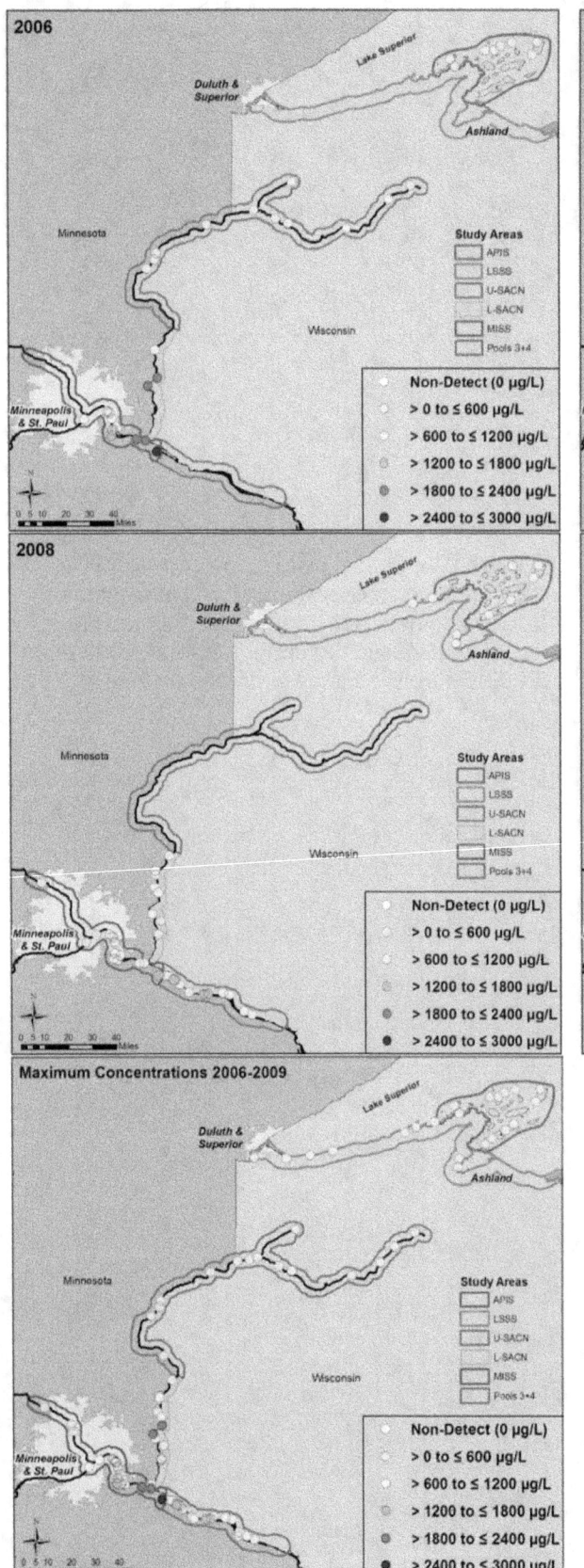

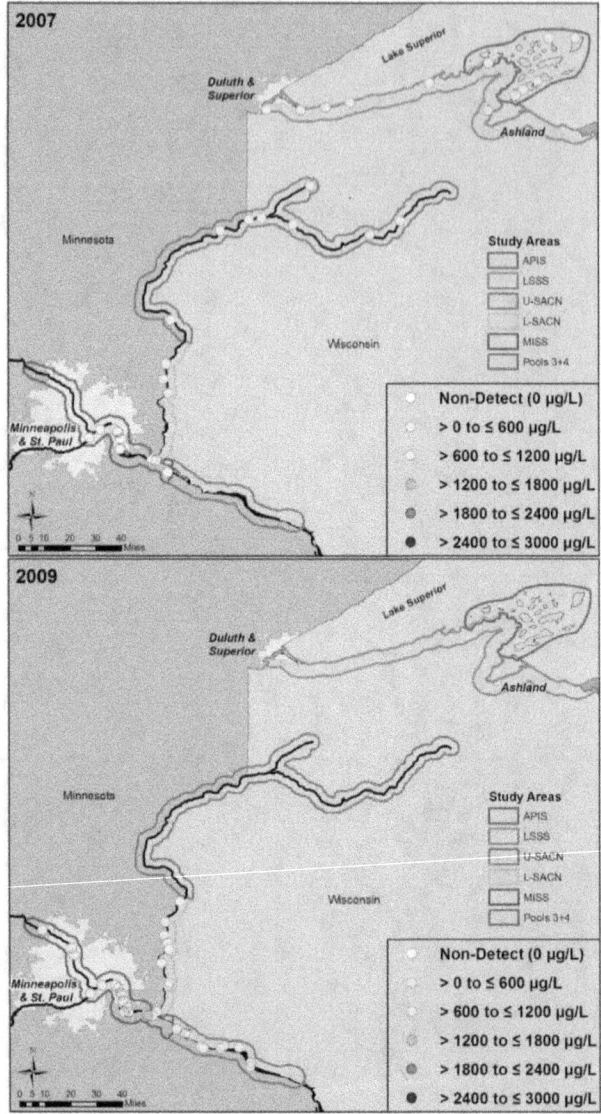

Figure D-9. Spatial distribution of total *PFOS* measured in plasma of bald eagle nestlings sampled at their nest from six study areas in the upper Midwest, 2006-2009. There is no known threshold value.

92

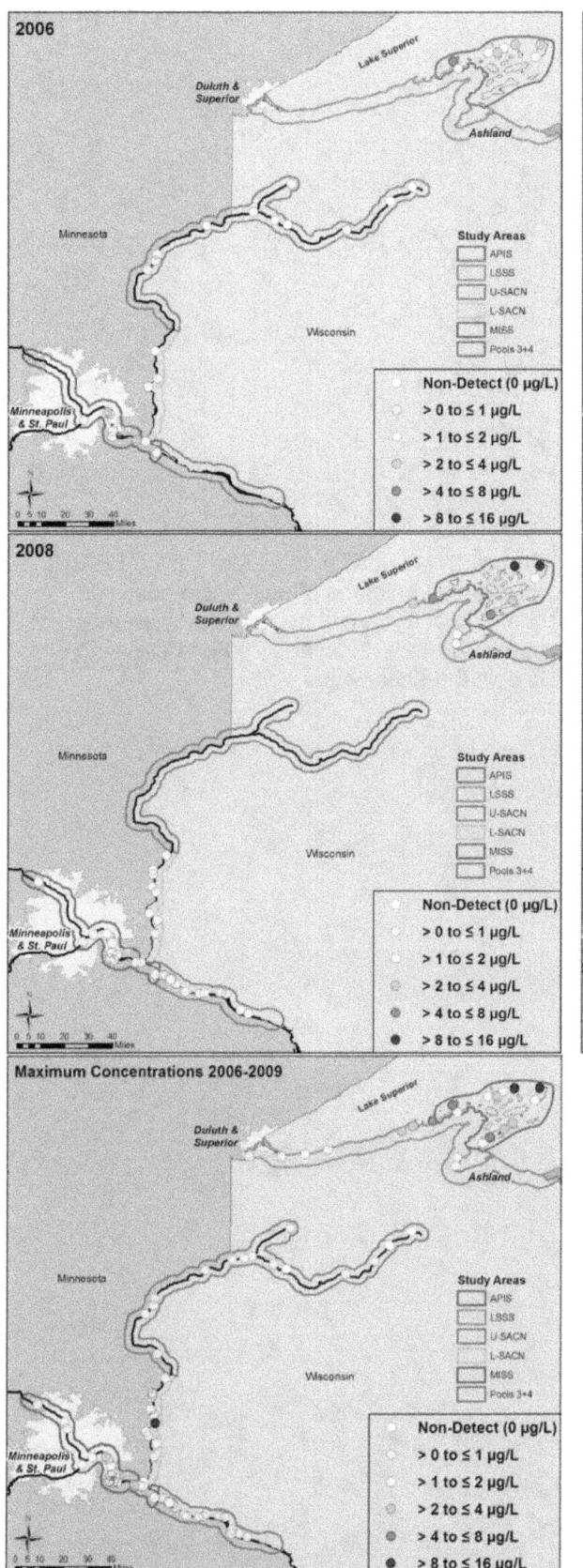

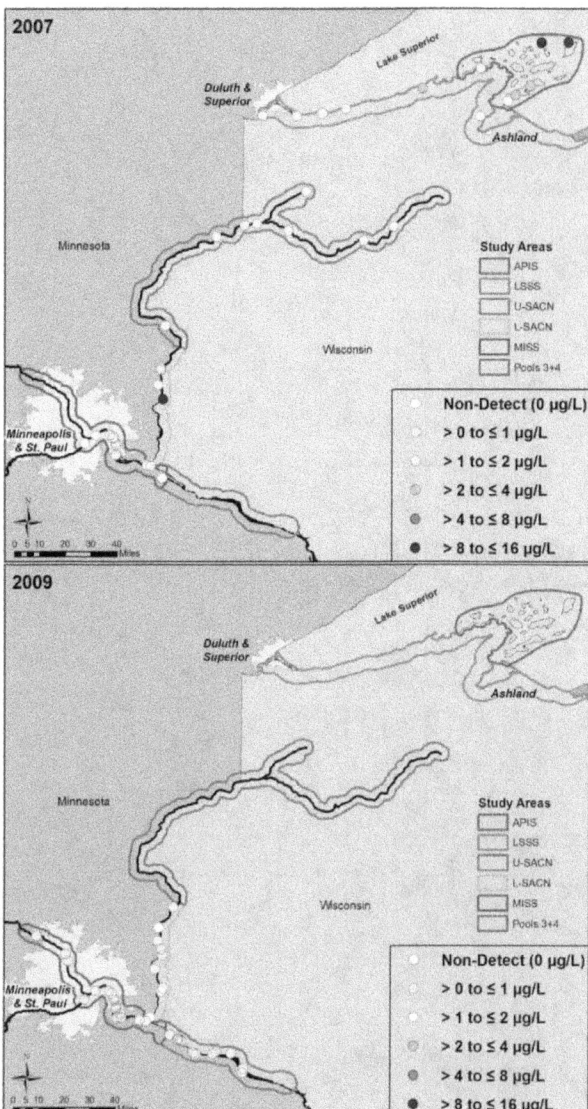

Figure D-10. Spatial distribution of total *PFOA* measured in plasma of bald eagle nestlings sampled at their nest from six study areas in the upper Midwest, 2006-2009. There is no known threshold value.

93

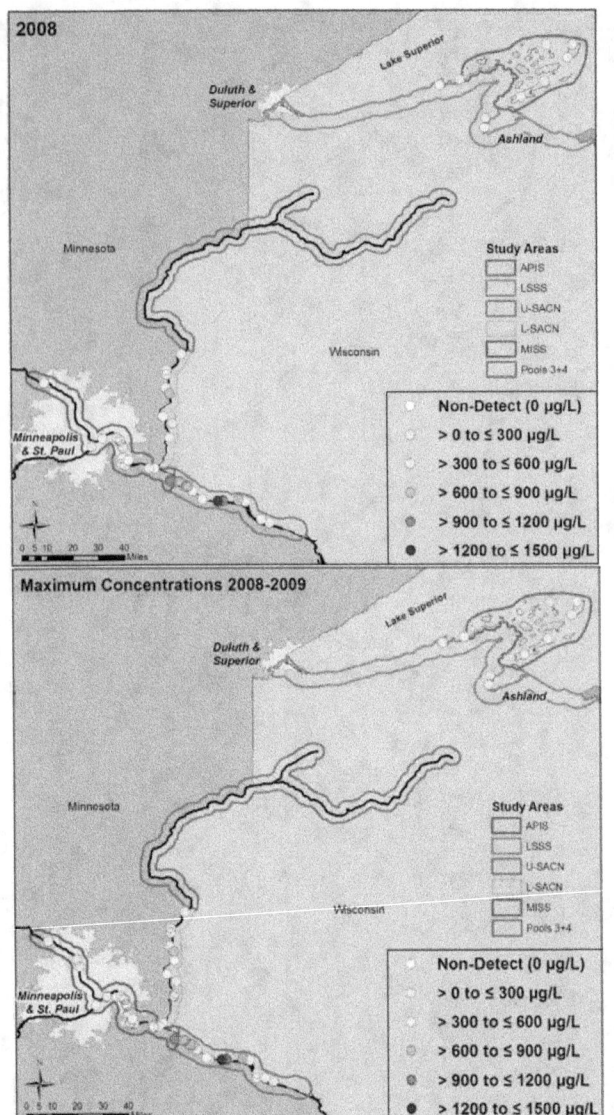

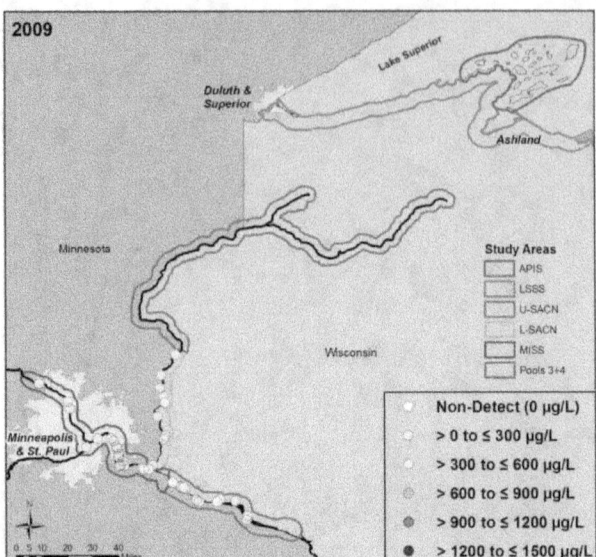

Figure D-11. Spatial distribution of total *PFDS* measured in plasma of bald eagle nestlings sampled at their nest from six study areas in the upper Midwest, 2008 and 2009. There is no known threshold value.

NPS 920/106819, February 2011